Word Processing with

Word for Windows

Be an expert!

GW00631116

£ 3-95

The *Be an expert!* series consists of books which enable you to teach yourself in an easy and straightforward way how to work with a computer program.

You simply follow the theory and the practical exercises and ... No trouble! It works! This series aims at being both pleasant and educational.

Also published in this series:
• Word Processing with Wordperfect
• Programming with QBasic

Anita Koelma

Word Processing with
Word for Windows

Be an expert!

Prisma *Be an expert!* first published in Great Britain 1994 by

Het Spectrum
P.O. Box 2996
London N5 2TA London

Translation: George Hall
Illustrations: Jurjen Tjallema
Production: LINE UP text productions

For the English translation
© 1994 Uitgeverij Het Spectrum B.V., Utrecht

ISBN 1 85365 341 1

British Library Cataloguing-in-Publication Data.
A catalogue record for this book is available from the British Library.

Contents

Introduction

As you probably know, there are different kinds of computer programs. These computer programs can be used to get various things done. Of course, things won't just happen by themselves; you have to know how to handle computer programs, which means that you will have enough work to do. Computer programs make it easier for you to work with the computer. They assist you in getting your commands carried out.

There are, for example, programs for making calculations and diagrams (these are called *spreadsheet* programs), programs for drawing and creating attractive pictures (*graphic* programs) and of course computer games. But that is not all: there are many more kinds of computer programs. One of these types which you will meet quite often is the *word processing* program.

Perhaps you have already worked with a program like this. There are various kinds of word processing programs (also called *word processors*). One of these is *Word for Windows*.

What can you do with a word processor?

As the name 'word processor' indicates, you can use it to process words. This does not only mean that you can type text; it also means that you can create text in the style you want and you can also easily correct any mistakes.

There are many kinds of texts, such as letters, school exercises, newspaper articles, advertising brochures, party invitations and so on. Almost everyone is involved with word processing in one way or another. For this reason, it would be very useful if you too knew how to operate a word processor.

Previously almost everyone used a *typewriter* to create neat texts. There is probably one still lying around in your house somewhere. At the time, typewriters were considered to be very useful, although they did have certain disadvantages. If you made a typing mistake, you either had to type the whole page again or you had to make good use of the correction fluid. And if you wanted to add something to, or remove something from, the text later, you had to begin all over again.

The invention of the computer and the word processor was a godsend. It saved a lot of time and even more paper.

What kind of program is Word for Windows?

Word for Windows is a word processor which is specially developed to run under *Windows*. What does this mean? Windows is a computer program which is easy to operate and also makes it easy to operate other programs. This is because when you have to make choices, all the options are shown clearly in small windows on the screen. By moving the mouse pointer to the option you want and then clicking on one of the mouse buttons (usually the left one), the command you have chosen is then carried out.

Therefore, if you want to work with Word for Windows, you have to have Windows on your computer. And of course, you need to have the word processor itself, Word for Windows.

If you already know a bit about working with Windows, you will know that it is a *graphic* program. In other words, figures and pictures are shown on the screen as well as text. We refer to these as *graphic symbols*.

In fact, Windows is not just a straightforward computer program; It is a graphic *system* which is used to
give the computer commands. Because it works with
figures and symbols it is clear and easy to operate.

Special programs have been written for this
graphic system. These programs are also graphic,
making them very direct in their operation. Due to
the fact that these programs have been specially
made for Windows, they all resemble one another.
If you know how to work with one of these programs, you will learn the others quite quickly.

Word for Windows is one of these programs. The
examples in this book are based on version 2.0 of
the Word for Windows program. If you have the
newer version of the program (called **6.0** suprisingly), you can still work with this book. Although the
more recent version provides more possibilities,
we are more concerned with teaching the basic
skills needed to work with the program. Whether
you have version 2.0 or 6.0, this does not affect the
basic skills required.

When working with some other word processors,
you type the text first and when it is completed,
you have to re-arrange it into the form you want.
But when working with Word for Windows you
can pay attention to the layout of the text right
from the moment you start typing. The screen
shows exactly how the text is going to appear on
paper. For instance, you can emphasize words by
making them **bold** (they are then printed in heavier
letters), or by using *italics* (they then lean forwards). You can also insert pictures into the text;

we shall do that shortly when creating an announcement about a class evening.

From now onwards, we shall refer to 'Word' instead of talking about 'Word for Windows'. That's easier for everyone.

What are we going to do?

This book will outline the possibilities of Word. We shall create all kinds of texts. Here is a compact list, just to give you an idea:

- writing a letter to a friend
- making an attractive layout for a school exercise
- correcting mistakes and changing text after it has been created
- making an announcement for a class evening
- making an invitation to a birthday party
- producing a school magazine and making it appear like a real newspaper.

1 Writing a letter

In this chapter we shall write a letter to a friend who has just moved away. We shall first start up Windows and take a good look at the screen. We shall then begin a new text and save it when it is completed.

Starting up Windows

In order to work with Word, you have to start up Windows first. You cannot start up Word on its own.

When you switch on the computer, the *DOS prompt* appears on the screen:

```
C:\>
```

Behind this prompt, you type the commands which are to be carried out by the computer.

Perhaps Windows will be started up automatically when you switch on the computer. This depends on your own computer settings. In that case the screen will look like this:

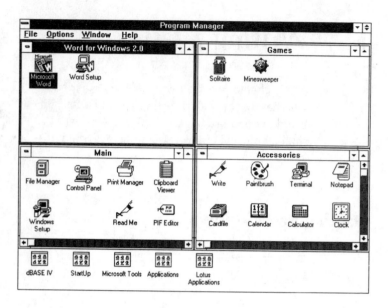

Your screen may look quite different due to the
fact that you can change and move the windows
and figures which appear on the screen. This is not
important at this stage. You can gain more information in Appendix A towards the end of the book.

If Windows has already started up, you can skip
this section.

☞   If Windows has not been started up, type the
    following command behind the DOS prompt:

    `win`

The word 'win' is the command for the computer
to start up Windows. Now wait until the Windows
screen becomes visible. This screen will resemble
the one shown above.

If Windows refuses to start, the best thing to do is ask for help. Your parents will probably be able to help. Perhaps another command may have to be given to change something on the computer.

Starting up Word

The Windows screen displays many figures with names underneath. If you have worked with Windows previously, you will know that these figures and names refer to programs or groups of programs which you can work with. You can start up one of these programs by selecting its figure or picture. These figures are called *icons*.

When working with Windows and Word for Windows, you will often make use of the mouse. This is often quicker than the keyboard. You can now use the mouse to start up Word.

Go to the Word icon. It looks like this:

Microsoft
Word

If you cannot find the icon, it may be in a window which is not visible at the moment but which nevertheless does exist.

In Appendix A towards the end of this book, you can find out exactly how the windows are operated in the Windows program. If you have problems finding the Word icon, read that section first.

We shall presume that you have found the icon.

If other problems occur, like suddenly losing a window, again the best thing to do is to read Appendix A. This deals with the solutions to this kind of problem.

Working with the mouse

We have mentioned that using the mouse makes it very easy to work in Windows and in Word. For this reason, this book will often tell you how to use the mouse to give certain commands.

When we refer to the *mouse pointer*, we mean the small arrow figure which appears on the screen. You can move this pointer by rolling the mouse back and forward across the top of your desk, preferably on a mousemat.

The mouse pointer is used to select something on the screen. It may also change its form, for instance, it may become a large capital I.

Sometimes we talk about *clicking* on something using the mouse. This means that you should move the mouse pointer to the required position and then press the *left* mouse button once, quickly releasing it.

If you are told to *double click*, press the left mouse button twice in rapid succession.

Getting down to work with Word

You can now start up Word. Move the mouse pointer to the Microsoft Word icon which is shown in one of the windows.

Microsoft
Word

Double click on this icon (thus twice in rapid succession when the mouse pointer is on the icon).

If everything has gone smoothly, the Word for Windows program should start up. The screen will look like this:

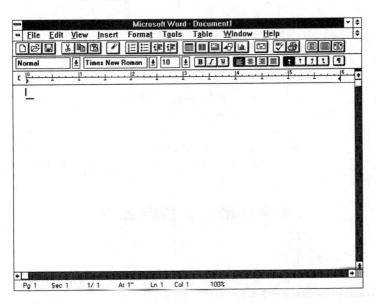

To summarize, Word is started up as follows:

- Start up Windows by typing 'win' behind the DOS prompt.
- Find the Word icon.
- Double click on the icon.

Typing text

On the screen, you will see an area in which you can type letters. The window itself is not completely empty; there are all kinds of words and symbols in the upper part of the screen; the work area where you will type your text is still blank.

The window can be increased until it fills the whole screen. This is convenient since you then see as much of the screen as possible.

It may be the case that the Word window does not completely fill your screen.

If the upper part of the screen looks something like this, it means that the window could be made wider:

Click on the small triangle pointing upwards at the right-hand side of the dark bar containing the words 'Microsoft Word'.

The Word window then increases to the maximum size.

If the upper part of the screen looks like this:

this means that the Word program window is as large as possible but the *document* window could be made a bit larger. (We shall discuss the term *document* shortly.)

You should then click on the small triangle pointing upwards at the right-hand side of the dark bar containing the word 'Document1'.

Now the Word program window and the document window have been made as large as possible. This makes working with the program somewhat more pleasant.

The Word program screen

The Word screen consists of many different components:

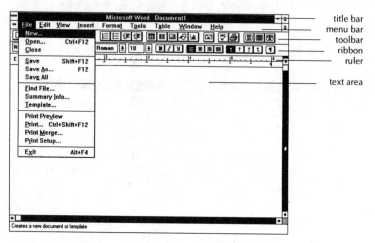

title bar
menu bar
toolbar
ribbon
ruler

text area

The **title bar** is located at the very top of the screen. This displays the name of the program (Word) and the name of the document (Document1).

The *document* is the text which you are working on at the moment. Each text as a whole is referred to as a *document*. If you want to save a document, you have to store it under a certain name. This is called a *file name*. For this reason, a document is also called a *file*.

The *menubar* is situated under the title bar. This contains the names of the *menus*. You use these menus to carry out commands in Word. These commands tell Word what it has to do. We shall discuss how to select menu commands shortly.

The *toolbar* is situated under the menubar. This toolbar is made up of various small pictures which are also referred to as *icons*. Each icon represents a command which can be given by clicking on the icon. You need to have a mouse to be able to work with the toolbar.

The bar under the menubar is called the *ribbon*. This bar works in the same way as the toolbar, but it is used to give different commands.

The *ruler* is located under the ribbon. This is used to place the margins and tab stops at the positions you want to have them. We shall deal with the ruler in more depth in chapter 6.

The largest part of the screen is occupied by the *text area*. This is where you type and organize the text.

Thus, the Word screen consists of the following components:

- the title bar with the name of the program and the document
- the menubar
- the toolbar
- the ribbon
- the ruler
- the text area.

You have had enough theory for now. Let's do something!

We shall write a letter to a friend who has gone to live in another town. It's too far to visit him regularly, so we send him a letter every now and then.

The letter we shall write will eventually look something like this:

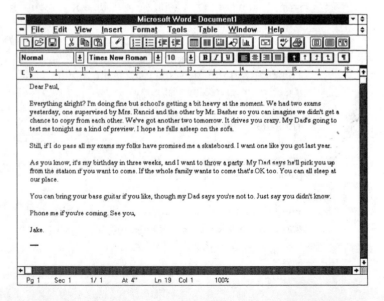

When you start up Word, you will see a flashing
stripe at the top left-hand corner of the text area.
This stripe is called the *cursor* or *insertion point*.

This insertion point shows where the text will be
placed when you type it.

When you begin typing, the text begins (not surpris-
ingly) in the upper left-hand corner where the cursor is located.

You will also notice that the mouse pointer has a
different shape in the text area. It looks like a large
capital I.

Begin typing as follows:

```
Dear Paul,
```

Of course, you have to type a space between
'Dear' and 'Paul' because it is normal to have a
space between words. And of course you have to
type spaces behind punctuation marks too (full
stops, commas, exclamation marks for instance) if
a new sentence is to begin there.

Then press the **Enter** key twice (this is sometimes
called **Return**). Then type the first paragraph of text
until you reach the empty line. Press Enter twice to
create the blank line.

You will notice that when one line is full, the text
moves on automatically to the next line. This is
called *word wrapping*. The program does this itself so
you do not need to press Enter to begin a new line.

Type the rest of the text as shown, pressing **Enter** to create the empty line where necessary.

Place your name at the bottom, 'Jake'.

The small flat stripe indicates the end of the document.

If you make a typing mistake

If you make a typing mistake, the best thing to do is to to press the ← key until the cursor is positioned just to the *right* of the mistake. Then press the **Backspace** key to remove the wrong letter. You can then type the correct letter.

You can also remove a letter by pressing the **Del** key. Move the cursor to the position just in front of the wrong letter and press **Del**. Type the correct letter.

Of course you can type a real letter to a real friend instead of this letter. Then you will kill two birds with one stone: you will learn how to type a letter in Word and you will give your friend a nice surprise.

The text layout

The blocks of text shown here are called *paragraphs*. Each paragraph forms a whole, dealing with the same topic.

You can move the first line of a paragraph a little to the right to emphasize it as you see in books and magazines. But paragraphs often just begin at the beginning of the line and are situated between two blank lines. Our sample letter is like this too. There is a blank line between the paragraphs.

In order to create this blank line, you have to press **Enter** to close the paragraph and then once more to make the blank line, as we already mentioned.

We shall now summarize these actions:

– The *insertion point* or *cursor* indicates where the text will be placed when you begin typing.
– The **Backspace** key is used to remove the letter to the left of the cursor position.
– The **Del** key is used to remove the letter to the right of the cursor.
– The horizontal stripe indicates the end of the document.
– Each paragraph is concluded by pressing **Enter**.
– You only need to press Enter if you want to begin a new paragraph. Word automatically wraps the words to the next line when one line is full.
– If you want to place an extra blank line between two paragraphs, press Enter one more time.

The other components of the Word window

We have not yet discussed all the parts of the
Word window. If you have typed this letter, the
window will look like this:

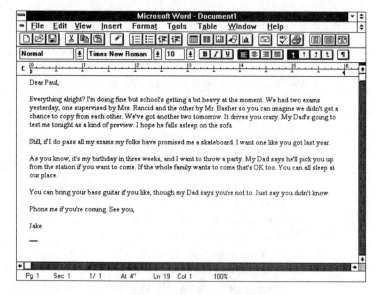

 There is another bar right at the bottom of the window, the *status bar*. This bar shows information
which can be useful when giving commands. If
you click on the name of a menu for instance, the
bar tells you what the first command in that menu
enables you to do.

In our figure, the bar displays information about
the position of the cursor.

Moving the cursor to another position

You already know that the cursor indicates the position where text will placed.

The cursor can be moved in two ways:

Using the keyboard: use the cursor keys ←, →, ↑ and ↓.

Using the mouse: move the mouse pointer by shifting the mouse across the top of your desk or computer table. Place the pointer where you want the insertion point to be and click the left mouse button. The cursor is then moved to this point.

In this way, it becomes very easy to insert sections of text. Perhaps you will discover that you have missed out a sentence or a few words when you read the finished letter. Just move the cursor to the required position and type the extra text.

If the text does not fit on to the screen

Sometimes the text is so lengthy that it does not all fit on to the screen. If you continue typing, the text shifts upwards off the screen. You can't see the top lines anymore. They are there, but they don't fit into the window.

If you have a lengthy text and you want to move to

a part that you cannot see on the screen, you can *shift* your text. This is very easy in Word. In this way, you can make any part visible on the screen.

There are two long bars at the right-hand side and at the bottom of the screen. The right-hand bar looks like this:

These bars are called *scroll bars*. They enable you to shift the text across the screen. That is done as follows:

  Click on the arrow pointing downwards in the right-hand scroll bar. The text will shift upwards and any lower text will become visible.

 Click on the arrow pointing upwards in the right-hand scroll bar. The text will shift downwards.

 Click on the arrow pointing right in the bottom scroll bar. Any text beyond the present right-hand side of the window will be moved leftwards across the screen to become visible.

Click on the arrow pointing left in the bottom scroll bar. Any text beyond the present left-hand side of the window will be moved across the screen to become visible.

Just reading this perhaps make it seem as if this is all very complicated, which it is not. Try clicking on these arrows to see what happens. Move the text back and forwards across the screen.

Using the scroll bars is very useful when you are working with very lengthy texts. This is not necessary with our short example letter since you can see the entire text on the screen at one time.

It is also very easy to shift the text using the keyboard. This is done by means of the following keys:

– Press **Home** to go to the beginning of the line.
– Press **End** to go to the end of the line.
– Press **PgUp** to move up one screen page.
– Press **PgDn** to move down one screen page.

Try pressing these four keys. The PgUp and PgDn keys only have effect if the text is longer than one screen page.

There are many more possibilities to move the cursor through the text using the keyboard. We shall not name them all right now, it's far too much to remember in one go. The four options mentioned above are the most important.

Document names

You see on the title bar at the top of the screen that the letter has the name 'Document1'. Each new document in Word is given the name 'Document'. When you begin another new document it is given the name 'Document2'. And the next is called 'Document3' and so on.

If you want to use a document again later, you have to *save* it. This means that you store it on a diskette or on the *harddisk* in the computer. If you have worked with the computer previously, you will have an idea of how to save your documents or files.

If you do not save a document, it will disappear when you close the Word program. You cannot re-cover the text. Mostly you will want to save the text, otherwise you have gone to all that bother for nothing.

When you save a document, you give it a special name. You use this name later when you want to use the document again. The program looks for the document with this name.

If you choose an obvious name, you will have an idea of what the document contains. For instance, if you choose the name 'letter', you will know later, when you are working in Word again, that this document is a letter.

In the same way, you can give other names to other documents you make, such as 'story' or 'exercise' or 'song' or whatever. This enables you to identify each document.

Therefore, the name 'Document1' has to be changed. This is only the temporary name of the document. When you save it, you give it a name of your own choice.

Summarizing:

– If you want to use a document (also called a file) later, you have to save it on disk.
– When saving it, you give it a special name.
– Document1, Document2, etc. are temporary names which are changed to names of your own choice when saving the documents.

We shall now deal with how to save a text in Word.

In this book, we presume that you have made a special *subdirectory* on the computer harddisk. You are going to store your files here. If you have not done that yet, the best thing to do is to read Appendix B first. This tells you what a subdirectory is and how you can make it.

For our examples, we shall use the subdirectory C:\TEXT.

To save a document, you can use a menu from the menubar. Remember what that is!

That is this bar:

To save documents (files), you need to open the
File menu. Each menu contains *commands*. When
you give one of these commands, the computer
will carry it out. Now you need one of the commands from the File menu.

Summarizing:

– If you give a command from one of the menus,
  the computer will carry it out.
– To select a command from a menu, you first
  have to open the menu.

☞ Move the mouse pointer to the word **File** on
  the menubar.

Click once using the mouse. This is the way to
open a menu. The commands contained in the
menu are then shown. These commands allow you
to do all kinds of things.

File	
New...	
Open...	Ctrl+F12
Close	
Save	Shift+F12
Save As...	F12
Save All	
Find File...	
Summary Info...	
Template...	
Print Preview	
Print...	Ctrl+Shift+F12
Print Merge...	
Print Setup...	
Exit	Alt+F4

If you have already made any other documents,
the lower lines in this menu will list some of these.

If you look closely, you will see that there are two
commands for saving documents: **Save** and **Save
As...**.

Remember this carefully:

– **Save** is used if you have saved a document previously. If you give this command, the document is saved in its present form under the
  same name.
– **Save As** is used when you want to save a document for the first time. You then have to give it
  a name. You can also use this command to
  give a document a different name. We shall discuss this shortly.

With our example, we are going to save the letter
for the first time, so we shall use **Save As**.

Move the mouse pointer to the words **Save As** and
click once. A new window will appear on the
screen.

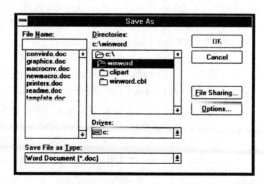

This kind of window is called a *dialog window* or *dialog box*.

Dialog boxes

You will often encounter dialog boxes in Word for Windows. These are small windows which appear when you give certain commands. In order to carry out the command, the computer needs a little extra information.

In this case, the computer knows that you want to save your letter, but it does not know which name you wish to give it. It cannot save it until you tell it the name of the document.

Saving the letter

You will now continue to save the letter. If everything has gone as it should, the **Save As** dialog box is now shown on your screen.

You will see that this dialog box consists of various parts. You will need to deal with the **File Name:**, **Directories:** and **Drives:** sections.

– In the box under **File Name:**, you type the name you want to give the document.
– In the box under **Directories:**, you select the name of the directory where you want to store the document. In our case, this is C:\TEXT.
– In the box under **Drives:**, you should let the

computer know that you want to store the **document** (file) on the computer harddisk. This is C: which has already been automatically chosen. But you can change it to A: for instance if you want to save the document on a diskette. In that case, click on the small arrow at the right of the **Drives** box. A drop-down menu appears. Then click on A:.

We are going to save the document in the C:\TEXT subdirectory. If you do not know much about directories, subdirectories or diskettes, read Appendix B before continuing.

If all has gone smoothly, a stripe will be flashing in the box under **File Name:**. This is also a kind of insertion point. When you type a name here, the letters appear directly in the box.

If this stripe is not at the position where you wish to type or change something, click at the proper position using the mouse. The stripe will begin blinking at the new position.

Make sure that the insertion point is flashing in the **File Name** box. Now type the name that you want to give the document. In our example, we shall use the name LETTER.

☞ Type the word **letter**.

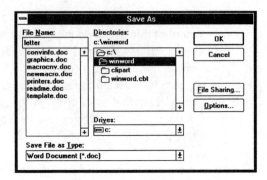

☞ Now move the mouse pointer to the **Direc-
    tories** box. This box shows the directories
    which are stored on your computer. For this
    reason, the directories on your computer will
    probably differ from those shown on ours. This
    is not important. We want to save the letter in
    the TEXT subdirectory.

☞ If no list is shown, double click on **C:**. The list
    will then open.

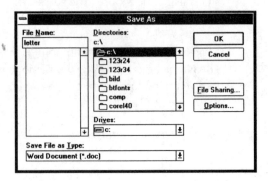

You will see a scroll bar here similar to those you
have already seen. If this is not shown on your

screen, this means that your list of subdirectories is
not very long and they all fit into the list shown.
No scroll bar is necessary to shift the list through
the box.

Find the subdirectory in which you wish to save
the letter. In our example this is C:\TEXT. If this is
not shown, click several times on the arrow pointing downwards until it comes into view.

Directories:
c:\
- dos
- hsg
- lotusapp
- pcw
- ps
- stepup
- text

When you reach the required directory, double
click on the name.

At the top of the box **c:\text** is displayed. This
means that the letter will be saved in this directory.

If you want to save the letter on a diskette, insert
the diskette in one of the diskdrives. You must
know the letter which refers to this diskdrive. You
can get more information about this in Appendix B
at the back of this book.

If you want to save the letter on diskette, you will
have to move to the **Drives** box. The diskette is always in drive A: or B:.

☞ Click on the arrow pointing downwards:

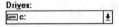

A list of all the diskdrives on your computer is
shown. Drive **C:** always refers to the harddisk inside the computer.

If you want to save the text in **C:\TEXT**, drive C:
will have to be chosen here.

☞ The proper choice is made by double clicking
    twice on the drive required. Normally drive C:
    will be shown here so you do not need to
    change anything.

The dialog box should now be filled in as shown:

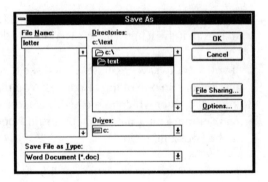

To actually save the letter, you have to tell Word
that you are satisfied with the way these boxes
have been filled in. To do this, click on the **OK** button.

☞ Click on **OK** (move the mouse pointer to the
   OK button and click once on the left mouse
   button).

A new dialog box appears:

You don't need to fill this box in. We shall skip it
so that matters do not become more complicated.

☞ Click on **OK**.

You will return to the normal Word containing the
letter. The title bar now shows the name of the document, LETTER.DOC.

Word places the letters **DOC** behind every given
name. The dot and the letters are called an *extension*. If you want to know more about file names
and extensions, read Appendix B. You are not
allowed to use just any letters and characters for
your file names. There are certain rules to which
you have to keep.

Summary:

–   To save files, you use the commands **Save** or
    Save As from the **File** menu.
–   The **Save As** command produces a dialog box
    on the screen in which you have to enter exact
    information.
–   When you are satisfied that the dialog box has
    been filled in correctly, click on the **OK** button
    to have the command carried out.
–   Word adds an extension to the name you give
    the document. The extension consists of a dot
    and the letters **DOC**.
–   When you give a document a name, you have
    to keep to certain rules (see Appendix B).

Using the keyboard

Key combinations

You have seen that it is very easy to work in Word
using the mouse. But sometimes using the keyboard can be just as handy or even handier to give
commands.

Often you need to press two keys at the same time
to give a command using the keyboard. We refer
to this as a *key combination*.

When giving this kind of command, you always
use the **Shift** key, the **Ctrl** key or the **Alt** key. These
names are shown on the keys on the keyboard.
There are two of each of these keys and it does not

matter which of the two you use.

In addition, the *function* keys are often used. These are situated along the top of the keyboard. They are called **F1**, **F2**, **F3** etc. If, for instance, you are told to press **F4**, you should press the function key and *not the letter F followed by the number 4*!

Have a good look at your keyboard to see where all these keys are.

When using this book you will also be required to use key combinations. If you are told to press **Ctrl-F12** for example, you should press the **Ctrl** key, hold it down and then press **F12**.

You will use the keyboard in the following exercises so that you will learn exactly how this works.

Click on the name **File** on the menubar. The **File** menu opens. Behind the **Save As** command, you will see the function key **F12**. This means that you can also press **F12** to give this command. In that case the **File** menu does not need to be opened. Pressing F12 opens the **Save As** dialog box straightaway.

Opening menus

You can also use the keyboard to open a menu when you want to select a command.

To open a menu using the keyboard, you always

have to press the **Alt** key. If you look closely at the
names of the menus on the menubar, you will see
that certain letters are underlined. These are the letters which are used to open the menu. Thus, to
open a menu, press the Alt key, hold it down and
press the underlined letter in the menu name.

Press the following keys to open the menus:

menu name	key combination
File	Alt+f
Edit	Alt+e
View	Alt+v
Insert	Alt+i
Format	Alt+t
Tools	Alt+o
Table	Alt+a
Window	Alt+w
Help	Alt+h

For example:
If you want to open the **Format** menu, press the **Alt**
key, hold it down and press the letter **t**. In that
case, we say 'Press Alt-T'. To open a menu, you always press two keys at once.

It makes no difference if you type a capital or a
small letter.

Summary:

–   If you are using the mouse and you want to
     give a command from a menu, you must first
     open that menu.

- Click on the name of the menu and then on the command.
- You can also use the keyboard: press the **Alt** key, hold it down and press the underlined letter in the menu name.
- Some commands can also be given using special keys or key combinations. These are shown behind the options in the menus.

When a menu has been opened, you can select a command. You will notice that one of the letters in the command name is also underlined. If you press this underlined letter, the command will be carried out.

You can also use the cursor keys to select a command. Press the ↓ key until the required command is highlighted or shown in a different colour. Then press **Enter**.

- To select a command from a menu when the menu has been opened, click on the command using the mouse.
- You can also type the underlined letter.
- You can also move the bar downwards using the ↓ key until you reach the command you want. Then press Enter.

Which version of Word do you have?

In this book we are working with Word *version 2.0*. A new version is regarded as being an improvement of the program. Each new version is given a higher number, for instance version 6.0, then 6.1 or whatever. Each new version provides new and improved options. This means that you can do more things using the program.

Let's have a look at which version you are using. If you are working with a version other than 2.0, certain commands may have a slightly different name. As we have already said, we are working with version 2.0 because this version is very widespread and because it is sufficient to learn the basic skills needed to work with Word. Some of you may have the newer version, which, suprisingly enough, is called 6.0, but you will also be able to use this book to get to grips with the program.

☞ Click on the Help menu in the menubar.

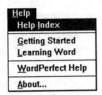

☞ Click on **About**.

A dialog window appears displaying all kinds of information about Word and your computer. The Word version is shown on the second line.

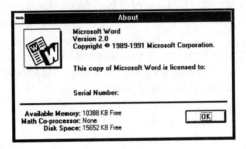

☞ Click on **OK** to close this window.

Closing the file and the program

When you have had enough of working with the program, it should be closed down. You **cannot** just switch the computer off, this may damage the program and you will certainly lose the current document.

You must first *save* your document. This has been explained in the previous section.

We presume you have saved the document in the
C:\TEXT subdirectory. You have given it the name
LETTER. Word now calls it LETTER.DOC.

☞ Open the **File** menu: Click on **File** in the menu-
    bar or press **Alt-F**.
☞ Select the **Exit** command: press **X** (which is
    underlined) or click on **Exit**.

You can also press the key combination **Alt-F4**. In
that case, you do not even have to open the File
menu. Press the **Alt** key, hold it down and press
F4.

The Word program will now be terminated. If
everything has gone smoothly, you should return
to the Windows screen.

2   Text layout

In this chapter, we shall deal with how to make the text look interesting or attractive. This is one of the great advantages of working with a word processor.

Word has many commands to help you make the texts as attractive as possible. You can even make them look as if they have been borrowed from a book. This process is called *formatting* or *layout*. We shall deal with text layout in this chapter.

You can do all kinds of things to and with text. You can print words like this:

in small letters
IN CAPITALS
bold
italics
underlined
~~strikethrough~~
in a different font
in a different size

Starting up Word again and entering text

You closed down Word at the end of the previous chapter. Now you wish to learn more about the program, so you start it up again. Remember how?

☞   Start up Windows if you have not already done so (type **win** behind the DOS prompt **C:\>**).

☞ Find the Word icon.
☞ Double click on that icon.

We shall use an English essay as an example in this chapter. Imagine that you have to write a composition about your favourite hobby. You have written the following:

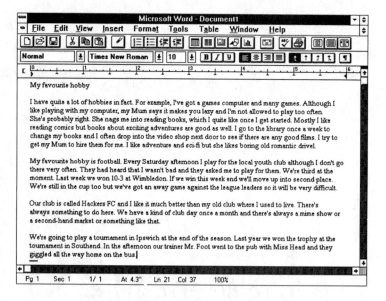

Type this text. You know that you should press **Enter** if you want to begin a new paragraph. Press Enter once more if you want to create a blank line between the paragraphs. The title is also a paragraph because you have also pressed Enter twice.

You may of course type any other text you like for this composition exercise. Perhaps you really have to write an essay for school; then you can type your own text instead of this one.

When you have finished typing, save the text:

☞ Click on **File** on the menubar.
☞ Click on **Save As**.

Or:

☞ Press **Alt-F**.
☞ Press the letter **A**.

Or:

☞ Press **Alt-F**.
☞ Move the cursor down until you reach **Save As**.
☞ Press **Enter**.

In the dialog window, type the name for the document: ESSAY. Save it in the C:\TEXT subdirectory.

If you're not completely sure how this is done, read chapter 1 again (see the section 'Saving the letter').

When the **Summary Info** dialog window appears, click on **OK**.

Filling in dialog windows

We outlined how to fill in dialog windows in chapter 1. We shall give a short summary of how this is done

— If you want to enter something in a box, click
on that box using the mouse. The cursor or insertion point will begin flashing there. Then
you can begin typing. For instance:

Insertion
point

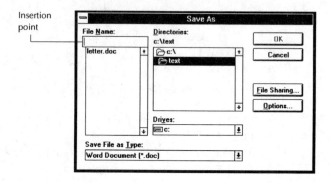

— If you have to select something from a list, you
can use the scroll bars to move through the list.
To actually choose one of the options, click on
the name.

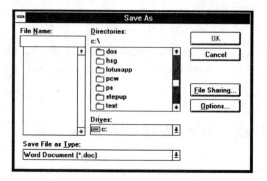

— When you are satisfied with the way the dialog
window has been filled in, click on the **OK** button to have the command carried out.

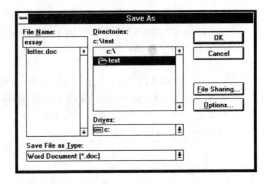

If you have given a command and a dialog box has
appeared, but you suddenly come to the conclu-
sion that you don't really want to carry out this
command, you can click on **Cancel**. The dialog
box disappears and nothing else happens.

If you like, you can use the keyboard on its own
when working with dialog boxes. If you press the
Tab key, the cursor will move to another section of
the box. Try it out.

☞ Press **F12**. The **Save As** dialog window appears.
☞ Press the **Tab** key a couple of times. Go on
until the **Cancel** button acquires a broad border. This means that this option is selected.
Press **Enter**.

Thus, you can use the **Tab** key to move to a different section of the window. When you arrive at the
right place, you can enter the information required
or press **Enter** to have the command carried out.

Try working with both the mouse and the keyboard. Sometimes the mouse will be quicker, sometimes the keyboard.

We shall generally talk about using the mouse in
this book since this is the most common way of
working. However, feel free to use the keyboard
whenever you prefer to do so.

The essay text layout

You can now get to work on the layout of the text.
This is also called *formatting*. The idea is to make
the text more attractive to the reader.

Making words bold

If the title were put into bold letters that would emphasize it a bit more. We shall do that. It is not
necessary to type it again; letters which have already been typed can easily be changed:

☞ Place the mouse pointer in front of the word
   'My'.

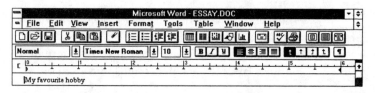

☞ Press the left mouse button and hold it down. Move the mouse to the right across the whole title until you have passed the word 'hobby'. Then release the mouse button. Normally we talk about: **Dragging the mouse** across or over the text.

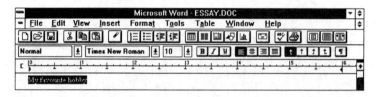

The entire title is then shown in a different colour or shading.

☞ Move the mouse pointer to the *ribbon* to the large letter **B**.

The B stands for 'bold'.

☞ Click once on the left mouse button.
☞ Click once anywhere in the essay text.

The title has become bold!

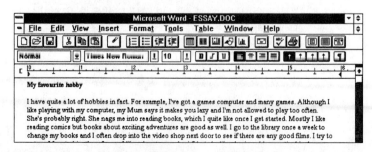

There is also another way of making words bold. We shall use it to change the name of the football club to bold letters.

☞ Place the mouse pointer in front of the 'H' for 'Hackers'.

☞ Press the left mouse button and hold it down. **Drag** the mouse over the words 'Hackers FC'.

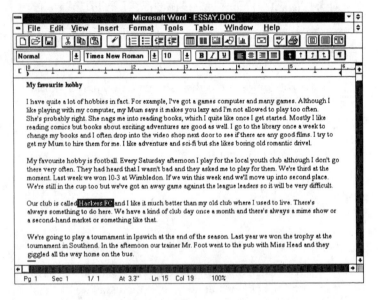

If the words are displayed in a different colour, you have done everything correctly. If so, go to the **Format** menu. If not, click anywhere in the text and begin again.

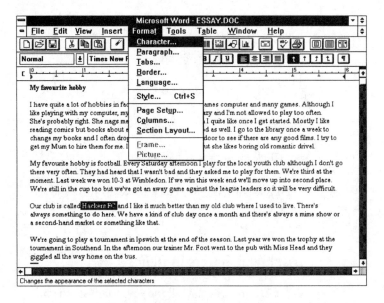

☞ Click on the **Format** menu in the menubar.
Click on the **Character** option.

A *dialog box* appears. This means that you can tell
Word exactly what you want.

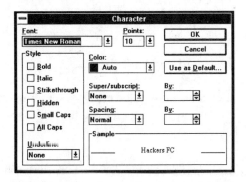

☞ Click on the small box next to **Bold**.

A cross is placed in the box. This kind of box is called a *check box*. The cross means that you have activated the Bold option.

☞ Click on the **OK** button.

The dialog window disappears again.

☞ Click anywhere in your text.

The name of the club, Hackers FC, is now shown in boldface!

Displaying letters in *italics*

We shall now display all the important words in *italics*.

☞ Place the mouse pointer in front of the 'g' for games computer. Drag the mouse over these two words. Click on the large capital I in the *ribbon*.

The letter I stands for *italics*.

Click anywhere in the essay. You will see that the words 'games computer' are now displayed in italics.

☞ Do the same to the words 'comics' and 'adventures'.

There is also a different way of displaying words in italics. We shall now discuss that method.

We shall display the word 'football' in the sentence 'My favourite hobby is football' in italics.

☞ Place the mouse pointer in front of the letter 'f' in 'football'. Drag the pointer across the word.
☞ Click on **Format** in the menubar. Then choose the **Character** option.
☞ Click on the *check box* in front of the word **Italic**. A cross appears in the box.

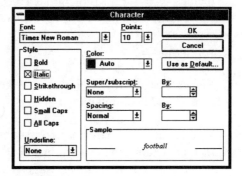

☞ Click on **OK**.
☞ Then click anywhere in the essay.

The word 'football' is now displayed in italics.

Marking words

You have learned that you have to drag the mouse pointer over words before making them bold or italics. This does not only apply to bold and italics, it also applies to underlining, or increasing or reducing the size of letters etc.

In cases like these, we talk about *marking* words or letters. This means that the words or letters are highlighted or shown in a different colour.

Practise doing this yourself and try changing the format of other words or letters in your text. If you have changed a word, you can change it back to its original state by marking it again and then choosing the **Character** option from the **Format** menu. Remove any crosses from the check boxes by clicking on them again. Then click on **OK**. You return to the text. Click anywhere and the changes will disappear.

You can use the *ribbon* to display words in **bold-face**, in *italics* or underlined.

You can use the **Character** option from the **Format** menu to change the word format in all kinds of ways. Try it out. Remember, you can always change back again.

Formatting paragraphs

We have dealt with the word format up until now. But you can also format entire paragraphs in one go.

Indenting

Often a blank line is inserted between two paragraphs so that it is quite clear where one paragraph
stops and the next one begins.

But this is not always the case. The text writer
sometimes *indents* the first line of a paragraph.
This means that the first line begins a little to the
right instead of at the extreme left-hand margin.

We shall now practise indenting the first line. It's
not usual to indent the first line of a paragraph if a
blank line is placed between the paragraphs; but to
learn how this works, we shall practise it in the following exercise:

If you want to format entire paragraphs in one go,
you can mark them as a whole. We shall now
mark the first text paragraph, which begins with 'I
have quite...'.

☞ Place the mouse pointer to the left of this paragraph, so that it changes into an arrow.
☞ Double click on the left mouse button.

This marks the *whole paragraph*.

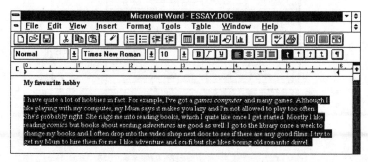

If you click too slowly or if you only click once,
only the first line is marked. But here we wish to
mark the whole paragraph.

And now you know how to mark a line: position
the mouse pointer at the left of the line where it
changes into an arrow. Then click once on the left
mouse button.

Keep in mind:
A *line* is not the same as a *sentence*:

—   In our example, the first *line* of the paragraph
    goes from 'I' to 'I'.
—   The first *sentence* of the paragraph goes from
    'I' to 'fact'.

☞   Click on **Format** on the menubar. Then click
    on the **Paragraph** option.

The following dialog box appears on the screen:

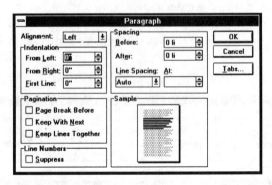

☞   In the *Indentation* box, click on the small
    triangle pointing upwards behind the **First Line**
    option. Click several times so that **0.5"** is

shown in that box. This means that the first line
will be indented by half an inch.

☞ Click on **OK**.

The dialog box disappears again and you return to
the text.

☞ Click anywhere in the text.

It will now look like this:

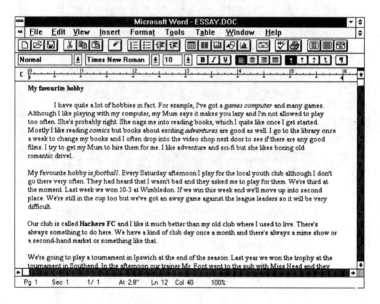

You can also indent the first line of all paragraphs in
one go. To do this, you must mark the whole text.

☞ Press the **Ctrl** key and hold it down. Move the
mouse pointer to the left side of the screen
where it turns into an arrow. The exact position
of the pointer does not matter as long as it is in
front of the text.

☞ Click once using the mouse while holding
     down the **Ctrl** key.

The entire text is now marked.

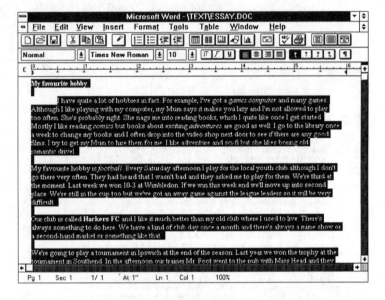

☞ Click on the **Format** menu in the menubar,
     click on **Paragraph** and change the setting in
     the **First Line** box to 0.5". This can be done by
     clicking on the triangle pointing upwards until
     the value 0.5" is shown. Then click on **OK**.

You see that the title has also been indented although that is not really what we want. A *centred*
title would be much better. In other words, the title
will be placed above the text, precisely in the
middle.

This is done as follows:

☞ Click to the left of the title so that the whole title is marked.

☞ Move the mouse pointer to the *ribbon* and click on this box:

Make sure you click on the proper box. There are four boxes which resemble one another, but this is the one you need. This is the one for *centring* text.

When you have done this, the text jumps immediately to the middle of the line.

Changing the line spacing

Another way of changing the format of the text is by making the *line spacing* larger or smaller.

The line spacing is the space between the lines of text. We shall now change the line spacing to Single. This means that the empty space between two lines is equal to the height of the text.

☞ Mark the whole text by pressing the **Ctrl** key and clicking to the left of the text while holding the Ctrl key down.

☞ Click on the **Format** menu and then on **Paragraph**.

A dialog box appears.

☞ In the **Line Spacing** box, you will see that Auto
is shown. Click on the arrow which points
downwards. A list opens from which you can
choose an option for the line spacing.

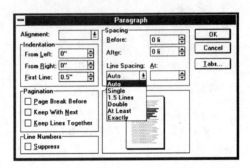

☞ Click on **Single**. A single line spacing means
line spacing equal to one line.

Click on **OK**. The dialog window disappears. Click
anywhere in the text so that the text is no longer
marked.

The result is shown on the following page.

Choosing another font

In Word for Windows, it is possible to choose
many different *fonts* or *letter types*.

When talking about fonts we are talking about the
shape or form of the letters. A font has its own particular shape and its own name. You can use a
chosen font to give your text a certain style.

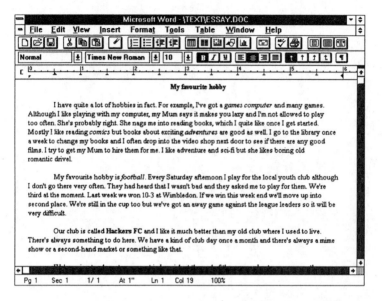

Generally, you will choose one font for the whole text, otherwise the text will look too untidy or chaotic. But sometimes it can produce a good effect if you use a different font to emphasize certain paragraphs or sections.

The size of the letters, also called *point size*, can also be altered.

The Word for Windows program only provides fonts which can be used on your printer so that the screen and the printout correspond to each other. Thus, the fonts you can use when working with Word depend on which printer is connected to your computer.

The size of these letters also depends on the fonts
you can use and the printer which is connected.

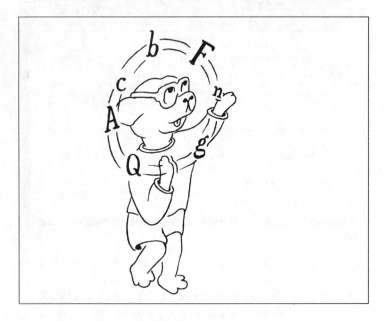

In the following example, if you cannot find the
font and the point size we are using, that does not
matter too much. Just select a different type which
resembles our example. The result is less important
than the fact that you learn *how* to change fonts.

We shall now change the font and the point size.

 ☞ Mark the entire text. If you no longer know
how to do this, take a quick look at the previous example.

You can also mark the whole text by pressing **F8**
five times!

☞ Click on **Format** in the menubar and then on the **Character** option.

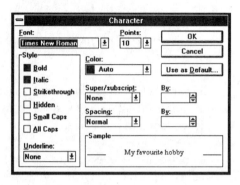

☞ Click on the arrow pointing downwards at the right of the **Fonts** box.

A list of fonts is opened.

☞ Click on **Courier New**. That is the name of a font.

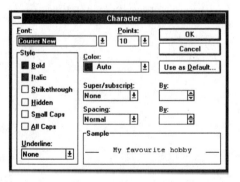

☞ Click on the arrow pointing downwards at the right of the **Points** box.

A list of letter sizes opens. Click on the scroll bar arrow at the side of this list to increase the numbers.

☞   Click on **20**. This means you have selected point size 20.

The **Sample** box in the lower right-hand corner of the window displays an example of the newly chosen font and point size.

Of course, these letters are much too large. We shall change the size once more. Open the list again and change the size to point size 9. Follow the same steps as outlined above.

☞   Click on **OK**.

The dialog box disappears. Click anywhere in the text so that the marking is removed.

The essay now looks like this:

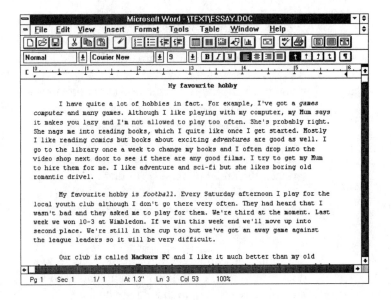

Saving the essay

To safeguard your work, it is a good idea to save it even though you are still working on it. Something drastic might happen: there might be a power cut, your brother might pull the plug out, your mother might spill her tea on you or the computer, your sister will probably delete the text while you're on the telephone. Then you will have done all that work for nothing!

You have already saved this document once (at the beginning of this chapter). You gave it the name ESSAY and Word added an extension, making it ESSAY.DOC.

First we shall now save the document under the
same name in the same directory. This is done by
choosing the **Save** option from the **File** menu.

If you have already saved the document previously
and you choose the **Save** option, no dialog window appears on the screen. The file keeps the
name you gave it (in this case, ESSAY) and it is
stored in the C:\TEXT subdirectory. It is in fact written over the previous version. **In that case, the old
text is lost**. This does not matter now because the
new version is the same as the old one, only it has
a more attractive layout.

But sometimes when you have made changes to a
document, you want to keep both the old version
and the new version. In that case, you should
choose the **Save As** option from the **File** menu.

Thus, if you want to replace the old text with the
new one:

☞   Click on the **File** menu and then choose the
      Save option.

There is also another method of doing this:

☞   Click on the *toolbar* on the following icon:

If you want to save the document under a different
name as well:

☞   Click on the **File** menu and choose the **Save As**
     option. Enter the new name in the dialog box
     which then appears. Click on **OK**.

Headers and footers

Texts can be made more attractive by adding
headers and *footers*. This is often done when there
is a lengthy text made up of many pages.

What are headers and footers? A header is a text
which is printed at the top of each page. This is
only visible if you actually print the text or if you
ask the program to show you how the printed text
is going to look. This is called the *print preview*.
We shall deal with this shortly.

You will notice that there is a header at the top of
each page in this book. This shows you the name
of the chapter on one side and the topic being
dealt with in that particular section on the other.

A footer is a text which is printed at the bottom of
each page.

We shall now give an example of how to place
headers and footers in a document. We shall make
a header for the essay.

☞   Click on the **View** menu in the menubar. Then
     choose the **Header/Footer** option.

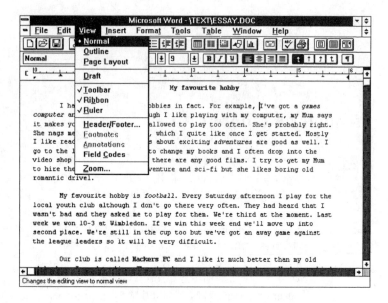

A dialog box appears.

☞ Click on **Header** if that word is not already marked.

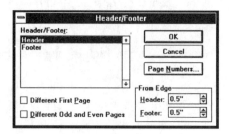

☞ Click on **OK**.

The dialog box disappears. The screen will now look completely different!

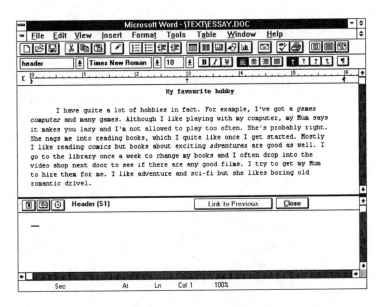

A new window is shown at the bottom of the screen. You can type a text for your header here, which, for example, has the following form:

```
English Essay - (date) - page (page number)
```

The '(date)' refers to the date. The date always refers to the present date, which means every time you call up or print this document, the current date will be placed here. '(page number)' refers to the correct page number. In this case, the essay only has one page, but if the text were longer, it would be convenient to have the pages numbered.

The *header window* has three *buttons* which can be used to place the page number, the date and the time in the header.

You can use this button to add page numbers to your header.

You can use this button to enter the date. The computer does this automatically from its own memory.

You can use this button to fill in the time. The time is adjusted in the same way as the date The computer does this automatically.

If everything has gone smoothly, the cursor should be flashing in the header window in the lower part of the screen. If this is not the case, click there once with the mouse.

☞ Type the words 'English Essay' and press the spacebar. Then type a dash (next to the 0 on the keyboard) and press the spacebar again.

☞ Click once on the second button to add the date.

☞ Press the space bar again, type a dash and press the spacebar again.

☞ Type 'page', press the spacebar and click on the first button to add the page number.

Relevant information is added to the header window.

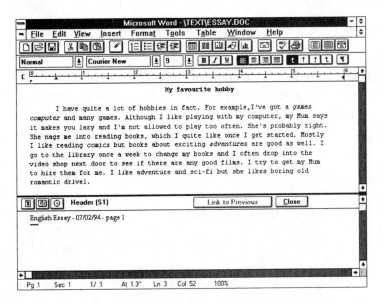

The header is normally placed at the top left-hand side of the page when you start printing. But in fact, it would be nicer to have it at the right-hand side, so we will *right-align* it.

Alignment

You have become acquainted with *alignment* when you positioned the title of the essay in the middle of the line.

When we talk about alignment, we refer to placing the text against the left edge of the paper to form a straight edge as in this book, or placing it against the right edge, or placing it exactly in the middle. You can also apply *full justification*. This means that the text has a straight edge at *both* the right and left hand sides. It seems as if the lines are of the same length, but if you look closely you will see that that is not so. The space between the words and also the spaces between the letters are adjusted to make the words reach the right-hand side.

This may be a little clearer with examples:

this text is *left-aligned*

this text is *right-aligned*

this text is *centred*

this text has *full justification* (we have made the text longer because otherwise you would not be able to see that the lines are positioned neatly underneath one another at both the left- and the right-hand sides)

Headers and footers can also be aligned. We shall right-align the header.

If everything is still working properly, the window containing the header should still be visible on your screen.

☞   Mark the entire header by clicking to the left of the text. The whole header should change colour or shading.

You can also click on the 'E' of 'English', hold the mouse button down and drag the mouse across the header. Then release the mouse.

☞ Click on the button for right-alignment on the *ribbon*:

The text jumps to the right-hand side.

Looking at the header

You are now finished with the header. Click on the **Close** button just above the header window. The normal document window returns. You can look at the header in three ways:

1. In the header window as you have done up until now. You can always change the header when you are in this window. Here you can type and delete text.

☞ Click on **View** in the menubar. Then choose the **Header/Footer** option. A dialog window appears. Select **Header** and click on **OK**.

2. In *print preview* on your screen. We shall discuss this shortly.

3. When you print the text. We shall discuss this shortly too.

Viewing the print preview and printing the text

If you want to hand your essay in, you will have to print it. Of course, it would be nice to get an idea of how it will look before actually printing it. You might want to change something at the last minute. You can get a *print preview* on the screen.

A print preview gives an almost exact example of how the text will be printed. This can also help save paper, which is always useful.

When you are completely happy with the print preview, you can proceed to the print commands.

Requesting a print preview

Requesting a print preview is easily done:

☞ Click on **File** on the menubar. Choose the **Print Preview** option.

The print preview is displayed immediately on the screen.

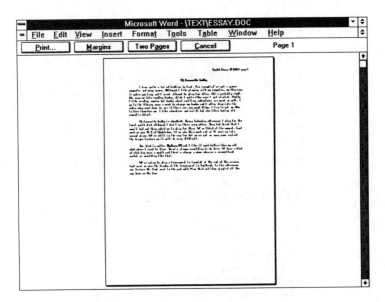

It is (almost) impossible to read the text. But making the text legible is not really what the print preview is for. The print preview is there to display the text *layout* or *format*. Is everything positioned correctly with nothing missing?

Of course, you can read and edit the text in the normal Word window. You don't need the print preview for that.

At the top of the print preview page, you will see the header you created. It looks fine. You can print the essay.

Printing the essay

There are two ways of telling Word to print the essay. You can do that from the window containing the print preview, and also from the normal text window in which you work.

If you want to do it from the print preview, click on the **Print...** button in the top left-hand corner.

The procedure is as follows:

☞   Click on **Print**.

The **Print** dialog window opens.

If everything has been installed properly, the printer which is connected to your computer should be named here. The **Copies** box should show the number 1. This means that one printout will be made. If you want to have two printouts, one for school and one for yourself, you will have to set the number of copies to **2**. This is done by clicking on the small triangle pointing upwards.

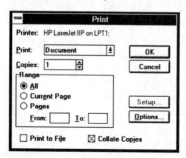

The rest of the dialog window need not be changed. The **Range** box shows that you want to print **all** of this document, which is true. You could say that you only wanted to print a certain part of the document, for instance only a couple of pages. But this is not a long document; there is only one page so leave the settings as they are.

☞ Check that the printer is switched on and that the paper is ready. If everything is in order, click on **OK**.

The essay will be printed.

If you want to return to the text screen, there are two ways of doing so.

☞ Press the **Esc** key.
☞ Click on the **View** menu in the menubar. Then click on **Normal.**

Page numbers

You have already added page numbers to the header. But you can also add page numbering without using headers.

Try this out.

☞ Click on **Insert** on the menubar. Then choose **Page Numbers**.

A dialog window appears.

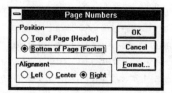

In this dialog box, you can choose whether the numbers are to be placed at the top or at the bottom of the page, whether they should be left- or right-aligned or centred. If you want to select one of these options, just click on the round button.

You do not need to add page numbering now because that has already been done in the header. For this reason, click on **Cancel** and the dialog window disappears.

If you do want to add or change the page numbering, fill in the settings in the dialog window and click on **OK**.

Saving the document and closing Word

Save the essay and exit Word:

☞ Click on the save icon.

☞ Click on **File** on the *menubar* and choose **Exit**.

You can also close the program down quickly by pressing **Alt-F4**. If there is a file or document you have not saved you will be asked if you want to save it before the program is terminated. This is an extra safeguard for your work.

3   Correcting mistakes and changing text

In this chapter, you will learn how you can alter existing texts after they have been created. We shall first deal with how to open documents after they have been saved and closed. Then we shall discuss the spelling check. And you will also learn how to make all kinds of changes in the text.

Making a text test file

In order to do the exercises in this chapter, we shall first create a test file. We shall use a letter with a few typing mistakes.

☞   Start up Windows and Word.
☞   Type the following text:

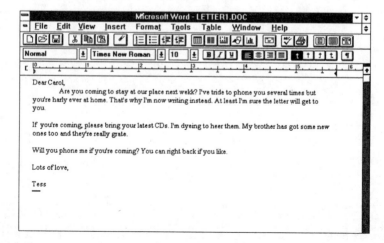

Make sure that you copy the typing mistakes so
that you can practise working with the spelling
check.

Then save the text:

☞ Click on the **File** menu on the menubar. Click
on the **Save As** option.
☞ Fill in the dialog window. Give the document
the name LETTER1. Save it in the C:\TEXT subdirectory.
☞ When the **Summary Info** dialog box appears
on the screen, click on **OK**.

Close the document:

☞ Click on **File** on the menubar. Click on the
Close option.

Opening a file

We shall now deal with *opening* files which have
been closed. It is possible for various files to be
open at the same time in Word for Windows.
When a file has been opened, you have *activated*
it and you can then work with it, or *edit* it as the
term goes. It need not be visible; perhaps another
window is covering it.

There should be no other file opened at the mo-
ment on your screen since you have just started
Word up. The only document that was opened,
'Document1', has been changed by entering text.

You have saved it and *closed* it. There is no open file at the moment.

You will notice that the menubar displays fewer menus:

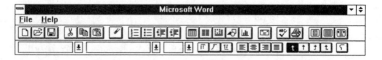

This is because no file is opened. In that case, there is very little you can do on the screen.

We shall now open the letter we have just saved.

☞ Click on **File** on the menubar. Click on the **Open** option.

The following dialog window appears:

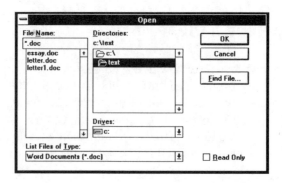

☞ Click on the file name 'letter1.doc' and then on **OK**.

The LETTER1.DOC file is opened.

If you cannot find the name you are looking for, this may be because the dialog box is showing the list of files in the wrong directory. You must make sure that the files shown are those from the C:\TEXT directory. The names of the directories are shown in the box under '**Directories**'.

If you do not see the name you are looking for, double click on '**c:**' and move through the list of directories, using the scroll bar if necessary, until you come to '**text**'. When it is visible, double click on it.

Correcting typing mistakes

The great thing about word processors is that you can use them to correct mistakes and to change texts.

Typing mistakes can be automatically found by the Word *spelling check*. The program checks whether you have spelled the words in the text correctly. The words you have typed are compared to a list of words which is stored in the program.

If you want to check your letter for spelling mistakes:

☞ Make sure that your letter is on the screen.
☞ Click on **Tools** on the menu bar. Then click on **Spelling**.

The spelling check begins immediately.

You can also activate the spelling check by clicking on the following button on the *toolbar*:

If you use this method, you do not need to use the
Tools menu.

A dialog window appears showing the first word
which Word thinks is wrongly spelled.

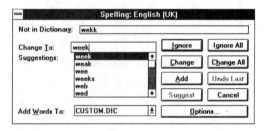

Word has found the word 'wekk'. This is indeed
wrong. You (we) have typed two 'kk's instead of
two 'ee's. A list of suggestions is shown. These are
ideas that the program has for the correct word. If
you see the proper word in the list, click on it. The
word will then be placed in the *Change To* box. In
this case, Word has already done that for us.

☞   Click on the **Change** button.

The word 'wekk' is replaced by the word 'week'.

The spelling check moves on to the next word

which it thinks is wrongly spelled: 'tride'. This should of course be 'tried'. Click on this word in the *Suggestions* list. It is then shown in the *Change To* box.

☞ Click on the **Change** button.

The word in the text is altered.

☞ Do the same with the words 'harly' (replace with 'hardly') and 'heer' (replace with 'hear').

If the correct word is not shown in the list of suggestions (you can move through the list by clicking on the arrows in the scroll bar), you can change the word by typing the proper word in the *Change To* box. If the cursor is not flashing there, click once using the mouse pointer. You can then use the **Del** or **Backspace** keys to remove the wrong letters. Type the proper letters at the appropriate places.

If you notice that you have spelled a word wrongly on more than one occasion, and you want to change it to the right word all through the text, you can click on the **Change All** button. In our case this is not necessary.

At the end of the text, Word will find the word 'Tess'. We know this word is written correctly, but it does not exist in Word's internal list, so the program thinks it is wrong. If you are really called 'Tess' (or in fact any name which does not exist on Word's list), it is a bit of a drag that this name is always picked out by the spelling check. But you

don't need to change your name! You can add the
name to a list of own words which Word will accept when it comes across them. The list of words
is called CUSTOM.DIC.

You can do this with all words which Word thinks
are incorrect although you know they are correct.
This is often the case with names. You can hardly
expect Word to know all the names in the whole
world!

We shall add the word 'Tess' to the list, the *custom*
list.

☞ Click on the **Add** button.

There is also another possibility when Word displays a word which is in fact correct but does not
exist in Word's list. Imagine that you do not want
to add the word to your own *custom* list because
you do not use the word often and adding the
word to the custom list means taking up computer
memory. Then proceed as follows:

1. Click on **Ignore**. Word will continue with the
   check and the word in question will remain as
   it is.
2. Click on **Ignore All**. If the word occurs more
   than once in the text, Word will skip it each
   time.

The spelling check is now completed. A dialog box
appears saying that the spelling check is complete.
Click on **OK**.

But just a moment! If you look closely you will see
that the words 'dyeing', 'grate' and 'right' have not
been corrected. Has Word not been paying attention when it should have been working?

Not really. Of course, these words are not correct
when used like this. But they do exist and therefore
Word has them on its list in these forms. That is
why Word does not see them as being wrong. Unfortunately, this means that you can't leave the
computer to do all the work; you will have to keep
your wits about you.

Move to the words in question and change them to
'dying', 'great' and 'write' by means of the **Del** and
Backspace keys.

Looking for synonyms

When reading the letter again, you might think: 'I
could have said that better'. Perhaps you would
like to use another word to express yourself in another way. You might regard some words as being
too simple or others as being too difficult. In that
case, you can get Word to look for *synonyms*.

A *synonym* is a word which has roughly the same

meaning as another word. For instance, 'drowsy' is
a synonym for 'sleepy'. When working with Word,
you can look for a synonym if you find a particular
word unsuitable.

In our example, we shall look for a synonym for
the word 'get'.

☞ Move the cursor position to the word 'get'. The
quickest way to do this is by clicking in front of
the word.

☞ Click on **Tools** on the menubar. Then choose
the **Thesaurus** option. A thesaurus is a diction-
ary of synonyms.

A dialog window appears:

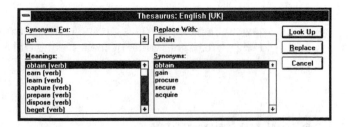

The word for which you are looking for a synonym
is displayed at the top of the window: 'get'. The **Synonyms** list shows a list of synonyms from which
you can choose. In our example, we don't want a
word meaning something like 'obtain' which is
shown in the **Meanings** box. Click on the arrow
pointing downwards in the scroll bar to see if we
can find a meaning which is similar to what we
want. Move down through the Meanings list by

clicking on the arrow pointing downwards in the scroll bar. You will see the word 'arrive' almost at the bottom of the list. This has roughly the meaning we want. Click on it. The words in the **Synonyms** box change. You are now given a list of words which correspond to the word 'get' in the sense of *arrive*. The word 'reach' is acceptable.

☞ Click on 'reach'.

It is placed in the **Replace With** box.

☞ Click on the **Replace** button.

The word 'get' is replaced by the word 'reach' in the text. Delete the word 'to' in order to make the text grammatically correct.

If you click on the **Look Up** button in the dialog box, the **Synonyms** box will display more synonyms which diverge a little more from the original meaning.

Try this out. Remember that you have to click on the **Replace** button to actually change the word in the text. Press **Cancel** if you decide not to replace the word after all.

Not all words have suitable replacements and many words do not appear at all in the list of synonyms. But there are probably enough to satisfy your needs for the moment.

Searching

When working in Word, you can easily search for and find certain words. This can be very useful when you are working in a lengthy text and you want to move to a position which is quite far from the current cursor position. It can be rather troublesome to have to look through the whole text for that one particular word you want.

We shall explain how this works, using the essay text which you created in chapter 2.

☞ Click on **File** on the menubar. Choose the **Open** option.

☞ Look for the ESSAY.DOC file name in the dialog box which then appears. Click on its name and then on **OK**.

Make sure that the cursor is positioned at the beginning of the text. If not, click in front of the first word.

☞ Click on **Edit** on the menubar. Choose the **Find** option.

Imagine that you want to find the word 'tournament' because you want to write another essay about football tournaments and you want to know exactly what you said here.

☞ Type the word 'tournament' in the **Find What** box in the *Find* dialog box.

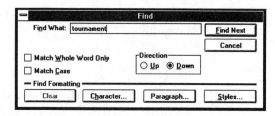

☞ Click on the **Find Next** button.

The word 'tournament' will be found. It is shown
in a different colour and shading so that you can
recognize it immediately. If you had the same
word further on in the text, you could find it too by
clicking on the **Find Next** button again. When you
have finished searching, click on the **Cancel** button. The dialog box disappears but the found word
remains highlighted on your screen.

Find and Replace

You can also replace words with other words.
When you have typed a text and are reading it
over, you might think that it would have been better to use different words here and there. You want
to replace them. Or you might have made a mistake and you need to change a word.

In our example, imagine that you have indeed
made a mistake. The football tournament is not
going to be held in Ipswich; it is in Norwich.

Make sure that the cursor is situated at the beginning of the text.

☞ Click on **Edit** on the menubar and select the **Replace** option.

A dialog window appears.

☞ Type the word 'Ipswich' in the **Find What** box. This is the word which is to be changed.

☞ Click on the **Replace With** box to place the cursor there.

☞ Type the word 'Norwich' there.

☞ Click on the **Find Next** box.

The word 'Ipswich' is found.

☞ Click on the **Replace** button.

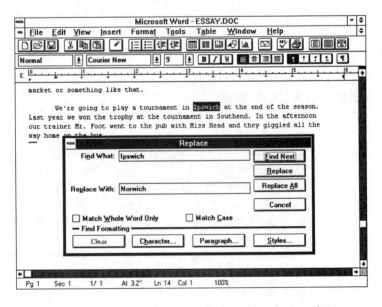

The word 'Ipswich' is replaced by the word 'Norwich'.

If the word 'Ipswich' occurs more than once, Word will move on to the next occurrence. In our text, there is only one 'Ipswich'. You can also see this by looking at the **Replace** button which has now become grey. The word 'Ipswich' cannot be replaced because this word does not exist in the text anymore!

If a certain command button is grey, this means that you cannot select it. This also happens with menu options or options in dialog windows.

When working with the **Replace** command, you can also select the **Replace All** option. This means that all occurrences of the word will be changed in one go.

☞ Click on **Close** in the dialog box.

This Find and Replace function can also save you a lot of typework. Imagine that you are typing a lengthy text about your football club, Hackers FC. Instead of typing this name each time, you could simply type HFC. When you have finished typing, move to the beginning of the text and open the **Replace** option (*Edit, Replace*). Type HFC in the **Find What** box. Type Hackers FC in the **Replace With** box. Click on the **Replace All** button. The proper name of the football club is automatically placed in the text!

As you see, the Find and Replace option is very convenient, especially in lengthy texts. You can replace words with other better or more suitable words in a quick and easy way. You can save yourself a lot of typework by typing short versions of words which often occur and then replacing them later.

Try it out. This is one of the great advantages of working with word processors.

Bookmarks

There is also another way of moving quickly to a particular position in a text. If, for instance, you have written a 10 page essay, you can use *bookmarks*.

A *bookmark* is a position in a text and this position is given a certain name. This makes it easy to move to the position later.

For example:

Imagine you have written a lengthy essay about pets. The first part is the more general part, the second part is about rabbits, the third part is about crocodiles, the fourth part is about stick insects and the last part rounds it all off. You can place a bookmark at the beginning of each section. Give the bookmarks the following names, for example:

first part	general
second part	rabbits
third part	crocodiles
fourth part	stick insects
fifth part	closing

Making a bookmark

We shall use our text about hobbies to try out this function. We shall place a bookmark at the beginning of the line 'My favourite hobby is...'. This bookmark will be called 'football'.

☞ Place the cursor at the beginning of this paragraph. This is easily done by clicking at the position using the mouse.

Make sure that the cursor is positioned exactly in front of the M for 'My'; otherwise if you click too far to the left, the line will be marked.

☞ Click on **Insert** on the menubar. Click on **Bookmark**.

A dialog box appears in which you can type a **Bookmark Name**.

☞ Type the name 'football' and click on **OK**.

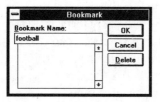

The bookmark has now been made although you cannot see it in the text. But you can easily find it.

☞ Move the cursor to the beginning of the text. This can be done easily by pressing the **Ctrl** key, holding it down and then pressing the **Home** key.

☞ Click on the **Edit** menu on the menubar.
☞ Click on **Go To**.

A dialog box appears in which a list of bookmarks
is shown. You have only made one bookmark,
'football', so the box only contains one name.

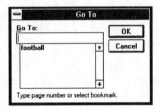

☞ Click on the word 'football' This word is
    placed in the **Go To:** box.
☞ Click on **OK**.

The cursor jumps to the beginning of the paragraph
'My favourite hobby is ...' where you positioned
the bookmark.

This function makes it very easy to move to a certain places in lengthy texts. Give the bookmarks obvious names so that you can remember roughly
what that part of the text is dealing with.

Save the essay once more:

☞ Click on the **File** menu.
☞ Click on **Save**.

4 Making a poster for a class evening

Imagine that your school has got something to celebrate: you have raised an enormous sum for the Red Cross by holding a sponsored rock marathon, or your school has been selected as a film location for Spielberg's new production, or something like that.

In this chapter, we shall make an announcement for a party in which several classes will participate. We shall try to make this poster as attractive as possible by paying close attention to the layout and by adding a drawing.

Working with windows

Because we are going to create a completely new text, we shall begin with a clean work area, a new document. It is not necessary to close all the other documents on which you have been working because it is possible to open different windows at one time in Word. The other documents are perhaps not visible, but they have not been closed.

Imagine you have been working with the documents ESSAY.DOC, LETTER.DOC and LETTER1.DOC. When you altered them you saved them just to be sure that you would not lose them, but you have not yet closed them by means of the

Close option from the **File** menu.

You can now conjure all opened documents on to your screen at once:

☞ Click on the **Window** menu on the menubar.
☞ Select **Arrange All**.

Your three documents are now displayed in low, broad windows. By clicking using the mouse, you can determine which window you want to work in. You can move the text through the windows by clicking on the arrows in the scroll bars. Although the screen is not very clear, it can be very useful to work like this if you want to compare texts or letters which you have written.

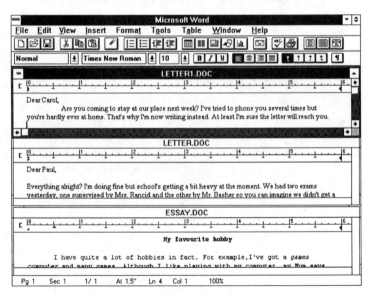

Beginning a new document

We shall now begin a new document. Word has not been closed down this time, so we have to start a new document as follows:

☞ Click on the **File** menu.
☞ Click on **New**.

The following dialog box appears on the screen:

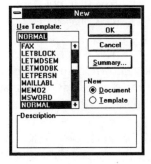

 This window is used to determine which *Template* is to be used for the new document. What is a *template*? You can regard a template as a *model*, as a special document style. The text is typed in this model. The standard setting is NORMAL and you have used this style up until now. This is fine for almost all kinds of documents.

There are also other templates. These can be used if you want to make a special kind of document: for example, a report or something in real letter style. If you choose this type of template, a number of things are placed on the screen automatically. With letters for instance, the places where the date and your name should be entered are already indicated. This can be very useful. When you have typed the text, you can save it as you normally do.

We shall now get down to work before it all gets too complicated. At least now you know what templates are and how to use them. If you want to try a few out, go ahead. To return to the original settings, you only have to open a new document (*File, New*).

We shall use the NORMAL template as usual. This is already shown in the **Use Template** box.

We want to make a new document so make sure that a black dot is shown in front of **Document** in the **New** box in the dialog window. If that is not the case, click on the word **Document**.

The dialog window should be filled in as shown in the previous figure.

☞   Click on **OK**.

The new document may be called 'Document1', 'Document2' or 'Document3' etc. That all depends on how many documents you have made up since the last time you started up Word. This name is not important because you will shortly give your new document a new name.

Adding a drawing to your document

We want to place an attractive drawing in this no-

tice for the class evening. This is easily done when
working with Word.

Make sure you have a new, empty window in
which you can begin a new document. Have the
new document fill the screen by clicking on the
small triangle pointing upwards at the right-hand
side of the title bar (remember we mentioned this
at the beginning of the book?).

Your screen should look like this:

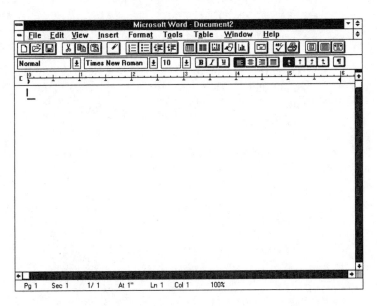

Your document may have a different number but
as we said, that is not important because it will receive its own name.

We shall now add the drawing we want.

☞ Click on the **Insert** menu.
☞ Click on **Object**.

A dialog box will appear looking something like this:

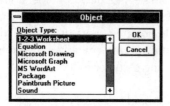

This window displays the names of a number of
programs from which you can import drawings.
Your screen may show different names because
other programs may have been installed on your
computer. Normally the program **Microsoft Drawing** will be listed here. This is a *companion program* to Word.

☞ Click on the name **Microsoft Drawing**.
☞ Click on **OK**.

You will have to wait a moment or two. Then a different type of window will appear.

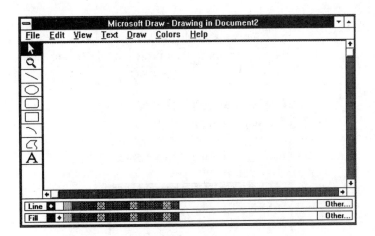

Click on the small triangle pointing upwards at the
right-hand side of the title bar. This will increase
the window to the maximum size which makes
working more pleasant.

If you like, you can create your own drawing here
in this window. This is done by clicking on one of
the buttons flanking the left-hand side of the screen
and then moving the mouse pointer to the drawing
area. Press and hold the left mouse button to make
the shapes you like. Release the button when you
are satisfied with the shape. Click on the Line and
File boxes along the bottom to apply the line thick-
ness and shadings you want.

This is something you will have to experiment with
in order to master it. Don't be too cautious, just do
it. You don't need to save your drawings if you
don't like them. If you are satisfied go to the **File**
menu and choose the **Save As** option to give your
drawing a name.

For our school poster we would like to have something which is ready-made because we want the
announcement to look professional. We shall *import* a drawing from elsewhere.

☞ Click on **File**.
☞ Click on **Import Picture**.

The following dialog box appears:

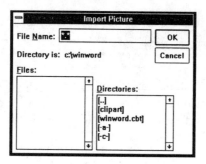

☞ Double click on **[clipart]**.

The **Files** box displays a long list of names of drawings.

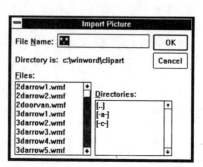

☞ Click on the scroll arrow until you see the **schlfish.wmf** file. Or just hold the left mouse button down to move through the list more quickly since this file is almost at the bottom of the list.

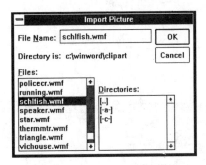

☞ Click on **schlfish.wmf** and then on **OK**.

Wait a few seconds and suddenly one of a 'school of fish' appears on the screen!

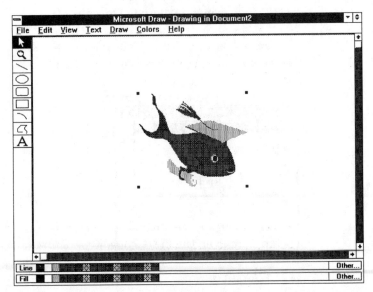

We shall now add it to the Word document.

☞ Click on the **File** menu.
☞ Click on **Exit and Return to Document2**.

If you were working with a document with a different number, that number will be shown here.

A dialog box appears on the screen.

We want to import the fish into the document, so you do want to update the document.

☞ Click on **Yes**.

The fish is imported into the normal Word screen.

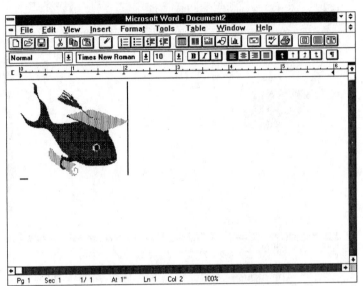

This is a fine specimen but perhaps rather large compared to the size of the page. We shall *reduce* it in size.

The cursor has become a very long, thin flashing stripe.

☞ Click using the mouse pointer at the cursor position, hold the mouse button down and drag the mouse to the left. Then release the mouse button.

The drawing has been *marked*. Now you can edit it. If you do not mark it first, you cannot change it.

☞ Place the mouse pointer on the small block at the bottom right-hand corner of the frame.

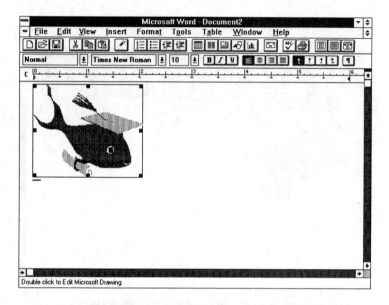

The mouse pointer now has a completely different form. It has become a dark two-headed arrow.

☞ Press the left mouse button and hold it down.

☞ Drag the mouse upwards and to the left until a new smaller frame has been drawn inside the large one:

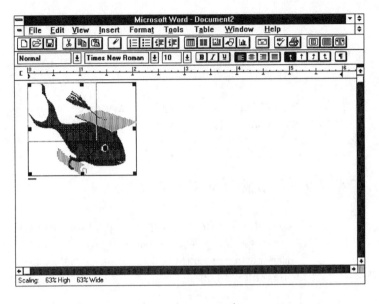

☞ Now release the mouse button.

The fish has become a tiddler. At least there is
enough space now to type some text.

Saving the document

This is a good time to save the document because
you have done quite a lot of work and it would be
a pity to lose it through an accident.

☞ Click on **File** on the menubar.
☞ Click on **Save As**.
☞ Enter the name PARTY in the **File name** box.
☞ Make sure that **c:\text** is shown under **Direc-
tories:**.

☞ Click on **OK**.

When the **Summary Info** dialog box appears, click
on the **OK** button.

If you have problems with the **Save As** command,
read chapter 1 again to refresh your memory.

Typing the text for the notice

We shall now continue with the announcement for
the class evening. Your screen will probably still
show a frame around the fish. This means that the
fish is still marked.

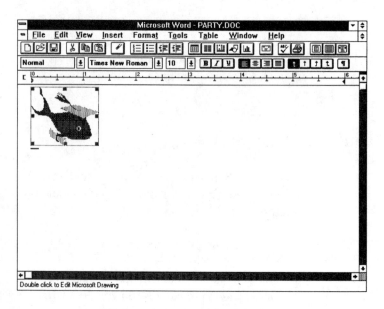

☞ Click to the right of the fish.

The cursor appears as a long thin stripe again.

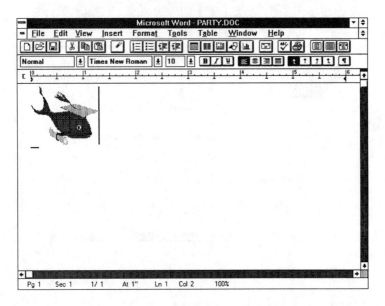

☞ Press **Enter** twice.

In this way, you ensure that the cursor position is moved down two lines.

☞ Type the text as shown overleaf.

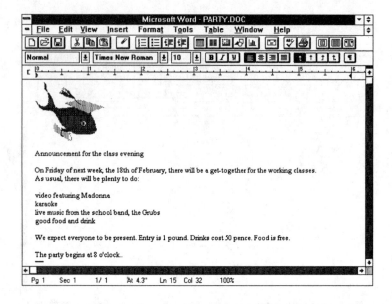

Showing all characters

As an exercise, we shall display not only the text but **all** the characters which have been entered in the previous document.

The 'extra' characters are not reproduced when the document is printed. They are only shown on the screen to assist you with the layout if you want. Two of these characters are shown below:

¶ indicates that you have pressed the **Enter** key.

· indicates that you have pressed the spacebar.

This example shows exactly how many times we have pressed the Enter key and the spacebar. In this way, you can see how many blank lines have been placed between the sentences.

If you want to see these characters on your screen, proceed as follows:

☞ Click on the **Tools** menu.
☞ Click on **Options** at the bottom of the list.

A dialog window appears. At the left-hand side of this window, there is the **Category** section. Make sure that the **View** option is highlighted. If not, move to it using the scroll bars if necessary and click on it once.

In the middle of the dialog window, click on the check box of the option you want in the **Nonprinting Characters** section. We want to see **All** nonprinting characters so we make sure a cross is placed next to this option.

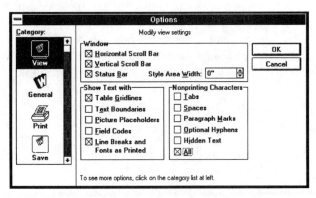

☞ Click on **OK**.

The characters you requested will now appear in
the text:

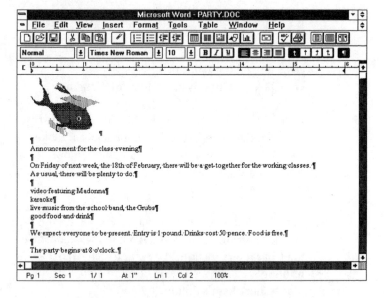

If you want to remove these characters once more,
click on **Tools** and then **Options**. Move the mouse
pointer to the check box next to **All** in the **Nonprinting Characters** section. Clicking there will
remove the cross again. Then click on **OK**.

The characters have disappeared.

The text layout

We shall now give the notice an eye-catching layout. It must attract attention when hung up in school.

Formatting the title

We shall first make the title **bold**. Then we shall change the font and the point size (thus the letter type and its size).

☞ Position the mouse pointer in front of the title 'Announcement for the class evening' so that it turns into an arrow. If it still resembles a capital I, move it a little to the left.

☞ Click once on the left mouse button.

The line is now marked:

☞ Click on the box with the large **B** on the *ribbon*:

The title is immediately changed to bold!

Keep the title marked, or mark it again if you have already clicked in the text.

☞ Click on the arrow pointing downwards behind **Times New Roman** on the *ribbon*.

Times New Roman is the name of the font which is now being used (see chapter 2). It is possible that a different letter is in use on your computer at the moment. This depends on the settings which have previously been made. This is not very important. In any case, click on the arrow mentioned.

A list of other fonts is opened. You can select one of these for the new title format. If you do not have the one we mention, simply choose another.

☞ Select Arial by clicking on its name. You may have to click on the scroll arrow pointing up-wards.

We shall now change the point size (see chapter 2 on paragraph layout).

☞ Click on the arrow pointing downwards to the right of the font size.

A list of font sizes is opened.

☞ Click on font size **12**.

If your computer does not provide size **12**, choose another, larger size.

You will notice immediately that the title is larger and is more accentuated.

Special characters

We shall now add special characters to the list of the evening's events (from 'video' to 'drink').

Four activities are listed. We shall place an arrow in front of each of these to make them more conspicuous.

☞ Place the mouse pointer in front of the word 'video', but make sure that it still looks like a capital I and not an arrow. This means that you should not position it too far to the left.

☞ Click once on the left mouse button. In doing so, the cursor is placed at this position.

The cursor is flashing just in front of the word
'video'.

☞ Click on **Insert** on the menubar.
☞ Click on **Symbol**.

A dialog window appears, enabling you to place
special characters in the text.

☞ Click on the arrow pointing downwards next to
the **Symbols From:** box.

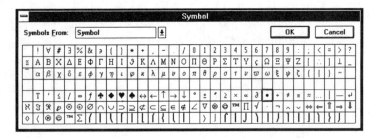

☞ Click on the name **Wingdings** in the list.

This is the name of a file containing symbols. Now
a new sheet of symbols appears.

☞ Click on the arrow pointing to the right, in the
bottom row. It receives a thicker border.

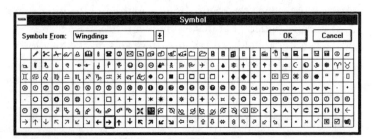

☞ Click on **OK**.

Do the same to the other three activities (karaoke, the band and the food and drink).

This section of your document will now look like this:

➔video featuring Madonna
➔karaoke
➔live music from the school band, the Grubs
➔good food and drink

Underlining

Finally, we shall underline the date, Friday the 18th of February, and also the very last line, since these are important.

☞ Click just in front of the F from 'Friday'.
☞ Hold down the left mouse button and drag the mouse across the word 'Friday'.
☞ Release the mouse button.
☞ Click on the **u** on the *ribbon*.

This underlines the marked word.

☞ Do the same to the date 'the 18th of February' and also to the last line 'The party ...'.

Printing the text

The text now looks like this:

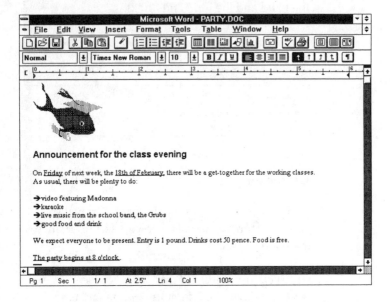

Read the text closely to see if you have made any typing mistakes.

The notice has to be printed of course if you want to hang it on the notice board at school. You should first have a look at the print preview to check whether everything looks alright.

☞ Click on the **File** menu.
☞ Click on **Print Preview**.

The screen looks like this:

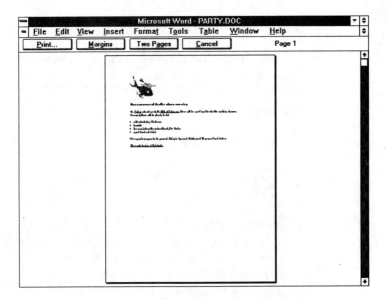

The text is very small, almost illegible. But you
have already checked it for mistakes so that's no
problem. It looks alright.

☞ Click on the **Print** button.

A dialog window appears. The correct printer will
probably be installed.

☞ Switch the printer on.
☞ Click on the **OK** button in the **Print** dialog box.

And, as you see, the announcement is just as you
want it to be!

If you do not want to print the notice:

☞   Click on the **Cancel** button in the print preview
     window.

Save the document:

☞   Click on the *Save* button on the toolbar:

You do not need to save the **Save As** option from
the **File** menu because you have already saved the
document under the name PARTY.DOC. You can
simply choose the **Save** command from the **File**
menu, or, as we are doing here, click on the *Save*
icon on the toolbar.

If you think that the notice is too small, and will
not be conspicuous enough, you can increase the
size of the letters. You can also choose a different
font. You must mark the text first if you want to
change the letters.

The Control Menu

When you want to stop working with this announcement for the time being, you should close
the PARTY.DOC document. This can be done in
two ways:

1.   Click on the the **File** menu. Then click on
        the **Close** option.

2. Use the document *Control Menu.*

We have not yet discussed the *Control Menu.*
There are in fact two Control menus, one from the
document and one from Word itself. They are
located in the top left-hand corner of the screen.
They look like two small flat blocks.

Document Control Menu

Word Control Menu

These Control menus enable you to give all kinds
of commands. They are opened by clicking once
on one of the blocks. These menus are often used
when working with different windows (making windows larger or smaller for instance), and for closing
a document or Word itself. We shall now use the
document Control menu to close PARTY.DOC.

☞ Click on the document Control menu button:

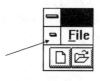

The Control menu opens.

☞ Click on **Close**.

The PARTY.DOC is now closed.

Make sure you use the lower Control menu. If you click on the upper button, the Word Control menu is opened. If you then select the **Close** option, the entire program will be closed down and you will have to start the program all over again if you want to work further.

If you do want to close down Word, click on the upper block and select **Close**. If any documents are still opened (LETTER.DOC or ESSAY.DOC for instance), and changes have been made since they were last saved, Word will ask if these changes should be saved. Click on **Yes** if you want to save the document in its most recent form. Click on **No** if you do not want to save these last alterations.

5   Making an invitation to a birthday party

We shall create an invitation to a birthday party in this chapter. This invitation will be sent to a number of friends. We shall do this in a special way. We shall use two files: one with the invitation and one with the names and addresses of your friends. When these files have been created, we shall *merge* them so that the name and address of a friend is automatically placed in each invitation. In this way, each friend will receive a special invitation with his or her own name and address. The text of the invitation remains the same.

Perhaps this all seems a bit complicated. But it is quite straightforward. You'll see!

Creating the text for the invitation

Begin a new document. We presume that Word has been started up, otherwise start it up now. If you need to refresh your memory, have a glance at chapter 1 again.

When Word has been started up, proceed as follows:

☞ Click on the **File** menu.
☞ Click on **New**.

Use the NORMAL *template.* This means that you
will have to make sure that the correct template is
highlighted in the **New** dialog box.

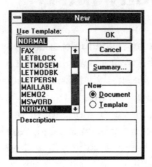

☞ Click on **OK** in the dialog window.
☞ Press Enter three times to create three empty
   lines and type the text as shown.

Save the document under the name SAILING.

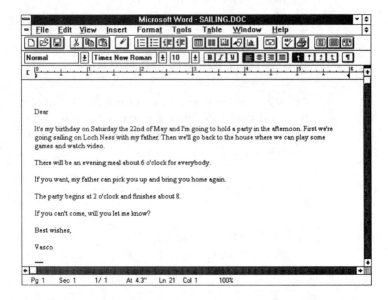

Remember how to save the document?

☞ Click on **File** on the menubar.
☞ Click on **Save As**.
☞ Type the file name: SAILING.
☞ Select the proper directory: C:\TEXT.
☞ Click on **OK** when you have filled in the dialog box correctly.

Click on **OK** in the **Summary Info** dialog box.

Do not close the document. We shall now display all the special characters being used in the text. This is handy for the next step.

☞ Click on the **Tools** menu on the menubar and select **Options**.
☞ Move the mouse pointer to the *All* check box in the *Nonprinting characters* section. Place a cross there by clicking on the box.
☞ Click on **OK**.

The special characters are now shown in the text.

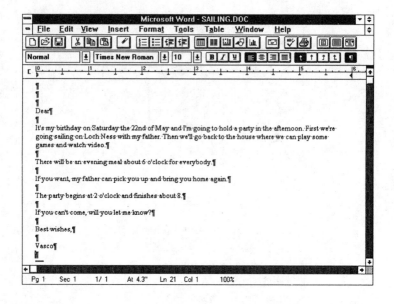

Creating a file with names and addresses

We shall now make a document containing the names and addresses of the friends who are going to receive an invitation.

☞ Click on **File** on the menubar.
☞ Click on **Print Merge**.

A dialog window appears.

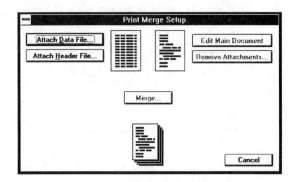

☞ Click on the **Attach Data File** button.

A new dialog window appears:

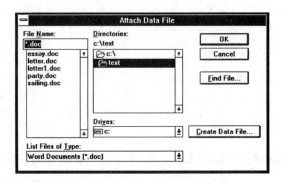

☞ Click on the **Create Data File** button.

Another dialog window appears as shown overleaf.

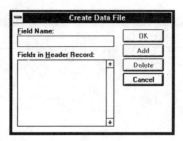

☞ Type the word 'address' in the **Field Name** box.
☞ Click on the **Add** button.
☞ Type the word 'name' in the **Field Name** box.
☞ Click on the **Add** button
☞ Click on **OK**.

The **Save As** dialog window appears. Save the file under the name ADDRESS1.DOC in the C:\TEXT subdirectory.

As soon as you click on **OK** in this dialog box, all kinds of things start to happen. The screen looks completely different. You can now begin creating your address file.

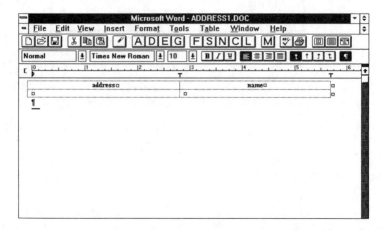

The cursor is flashing under **address**. Type the
name and address of a friend you want to invite:

☞ Type 'Walter Rally'.
☞ Press **Enter**.
☞ Type '1 Cloak Crossing'.
☞ Press **Enter** again.
☞ Type 'Inverness IN4 1ER'.
☞ press the **Tab** key.
☞ Type 'Walt'.
☞ Press the **Tab** key.

The screen should look like this:

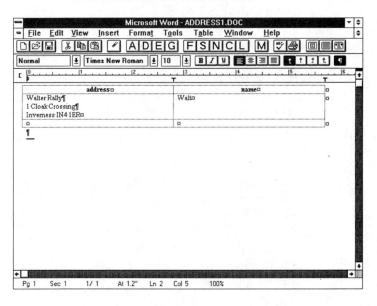

You have now typed the name and address for one
person. Do the same for the rest of your friends.
Type their names and addresses just as you have
done with Walter. To move from the left-hand field
(address) to the right-hand field (name), press the

Tab key. You also press the **Tab** key to move from the *name* field to the next *address* field. A *field* can be described as being a kind of unit within a document.

Fill in the names and addresses of your friends as follows (of course, you can type the names of your own friends):

address	**name**
Frances Drake 2 Bowling Lane Inverness IN3 6NS	Frances
Horatio Nilson 18 Trafalgar Square Fort William FW2 4KM	Horry
James Cooke 5 Aboriginal View Fort Augustus FA 5JN	Jim
William Bly 43 Bounty Blvrd Beauly BL9 8BR	Billy
Henry Morgan 13 Jolly Rodger Row Urquhart UR6 2WE	Henk

You do not need to press the **Tab** key after typing the last information. The screen now looks like this:

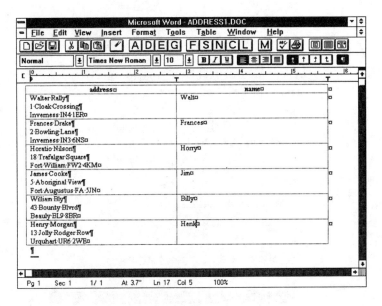

☞ Click on the **File** menu.

☞ Click on **Save**.

Click on **OK** when the **Summary Info** dialog box appears.

Merging the documents

The invitation and the address document are now to be merged so that each person will receive a separate invitation with his/her own name and address. Only the invitation text itself is identical in all cases.

☞ Click on the **Window** menu on the menubar.

☞ Click on the **SAILING.DOC** at the bottom of the options.

In this way it is possible to switch to the text of the
invitation which you saved in the SAILING.DOC.

When the SAILING.DOC text appears on your
screen, proceed as follows:

☞ Press the **Ctrl** and the **Home** keys at the same
time to move to the beginning of the document.
☞ Click on the **Insert Merge Field** button above
the *ruler*.

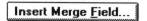

The following dialog box appears:

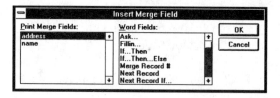

☞ Click on **address**.
☞ Click on **OK**.

You will see that **<<address>>** appears at the top
of the text. This means that the information that
you have entered in the ADDRESS.DOC will be
placed here. We refer to this as a *field*. Something
different is placed in this field in each letter. You
have filled in different information for each person.

The 'address' field also contains the full name, but
we have called it 'address' because that is where
the letter will be sent. We also have the 'name'

field which is used to greet your friend personally.

☞ Click right behind the word 'Dear' in the text.
☞ Press the spacebar to make a little room.
☞ Click on the **Insert Merge Field** button.
☞ Click on **name** in the dialog window.
☞ Click on **OK**.

You will see that **<<name>>** has been placed behind 'Dear'. This is also a *field*. A different name will be placed here in each letter.

☞ Type a comma behind **<<name>>**.

The screen looks like this:

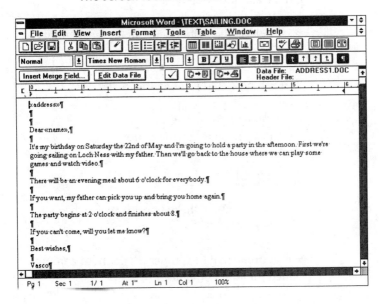

Save SAILING.DOC once more:

☞ Click on **File** on the menubar.

☞ Click on **Save**.

You can now begin merging the documents. Before you actually begin printing the invitations, click on the following button:

A new document with the name **Form Letters1** appears on the screen. This contains all the invitations to your friends. You can browse through this document just as you can with all other files. Use the scroll bars or the cursor keys to do this.

Go back to the document:

☞ Click on the **Window** menu on the menubar.
☞ Click on **SAILING.DOC**.

You can now start printing the invitations:

☞ Switch on the printer.
☞ Click on the following button:

☞ Click on **OK** in the dialog box which then appears.

We presume that the proper printer has been installed for your computer.

You will have to wait a little. Word needs time to merge all the invitations and to print them, but within a short period, six perfect invitations will be produced.

If you want, you can improve the layout of the invitations by increasing the size of some letters or by making certain sections bold or underlining them for instance. This is entirely up to you. If you want to do this, make the changes in the text *before* it is merged with the addresses. In that case, you only need to make the changes once.

When you have finished, save your documents, ADDRESS.DOC and SAILING.DOC, and close them.

If you want, you can also save the Form Letters1 document too. Give it a different name, INVI-TATN.DOC for example.

If you need help

If you're stuck and can't get any further, Word can help you. Word provides a companion program which can give you information about all kinds of commands.

Follow these exercises so you will learn how it works.

Starting the Help program

The Help program is started up by opening the **Help** menu.

☞ Click on **Help** on the menubar.

The Help program menu is opened. Select *Help Index*.

☞ Click on **Help Index**.

The following appears on the screen:

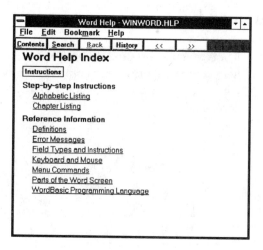

The lines which are underlined are *topics*. You can gain more information about any of these by selecting it. The easiest way of doing this is by clicking on it using the mouse. You can also press the **Tab** key to move through the topics. Then press the **Enter** key to get the information.

Try this out. Select the **Definitions** topic.

☞ Click on **Definitions**.

☞ Or press the **Tab** key until the word *Definitions* is shown in a different colour.

If you are using the mouse, a new screen is opened immediately.

If you are using the **Tab** key, nothing will happen at first. You have to press the **Enter** key to open the topic which has been highlighted.

When you have done this, the following screen will appear:

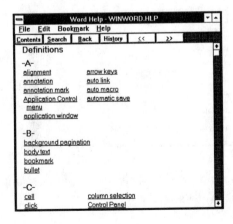

A list of difficult words is shown. These words are often used in Word, especially in dialog windows

and commands. For this reason, it is advisable to
know what they mean.

You can choose any word from the list. For
example, we shall choose the term **dialog box**.

☞ Move the mouse pointer to the right scroll bar
    and click on the arrow pointing downwards
    until the term **dialog box** becomes visible.

If you then move the mouse pointer to this term,
the arrow changes into a hand with a pointing
finger. Click on the left mouse button. You can
also move to this term by pressing the **Tab** key and
then **Enter**.

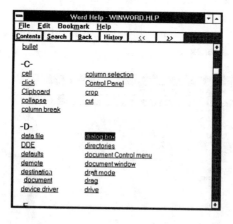

A window will appear with a short explanation
about dialog boxes.

Close the Help function:

☞ Click on the **File** menu of *Word Help*.

☞ Click on **Exit**.

Using the F1 key

You can also get help without first having to open
the Help menu. This is done by pressing the **F1** key.
Imagine that you want to use the **Print Merge** command but you would like to know more about it before beginning.

Proceed as follows:

☞ Click on the **File** menu.
☞ Use the *cursor key* to move to the **Print Merge**
    command. Make sure that it is highlighted.
    Thus, *do not* click on it with the mouse!
☞ Press the **F1** key.

A whole screen full of information will be displayed.
This tells you how to work with this command. If you
now click on an underlined word or term, a new
screen with new information will appear. If you click
on a word which is underlined with a broken line, an
explanation of that word will be given.

You can move through the text using the scroll
bars or the cursor keys.

If you need help when filling in a dialog box, press
F1 when the dialog box is shown on the screen.

When you close the Help file again, you will return to the normal dialog window where you left
off.

The Help function is very easy to use. You can find lots of information to help you if you get stuck. You can also gain information about the toolbar, the ribbon and the ruler. Try it out. Nothing can go wrong and practice makes perfect.

6   Making the school magazine

Because of your literary talents, you have been asked to take charge of the school magazine. It will resemble a real newspaper.

The text will be typed first and then attention will be given to the layout.

The school magazine in this chapter may not resemble the school magazine as you know it, but it is of course only meant to be an example.

Typing the text for the magazine

First open a new document to type the new text.
Do not use the **File** menu this time; use the *toolbar*
for a change. If you click on this icon, a new document is opened which uses a NORMAL template.
This is what we want in this case.

☞ Click on the following button on the *toolbar*:

An empty document with the name 'Document1'
or 'Document2' appears on the screen. This of
course depends on the documents you have created up until now.

☞ Type the following text in the new document:

```
The Glossy magazine
Gloucester High school newspaper


Sports day a great success

The communal sports day, held in conjunction
with five other local schools, turned out to be
a great success. Our school in particular had a
field day as one might say. The school football
team won all its matches just like last year and
it will be no surprise if the playground is soon
full with chequebook-waving scouts. The hockey
```

team was less successful but managed to reach fifth place. Our athletes gave a fantastic performance. Chris Linford came first in the individual competition with Jack Colinson a good second. The relay team, rather bloated with too much pie, pudding and lemonade, came a disappointing third.

Next year the annual sports day will be held in the grounds of the St. Gazza School for Wayward Children.

Class Evening

Class 1E will hold another party next week, on Friday the 13th of May. This will be the sixth party this year. They don't seem to be able to get enough of it. The other first year classes are also invited. The evening program is as follows:

-video with Arnold Schwarzenegger
-karaoke
-live band
-food and drink.

It is still a secret which band is going to play. But the organisers have promised that it will be a spectacular evening. Entry will cost £1, drinks 50 pence and victuals are free. The party begins at 8 o'clock. Bring your dancing shoes/trousers.

Farewell to Mrs Erring

Our cookery teacher, Mrs Kate Erring, will take
her leave of us on Friday the 20th of May. She
has accepted a job on the Cunard line to the
South Pole. She is at present experimenting with
new recipes for penguin. A farewell speech will
be held in the canteen by Mr Basher the
headmaster. A reception will follow on. All
third and fourth year pupils are welcome.

New teachers

Since the first of this month, our school has
two new teachers:

Mrs Boyle-Degg, cookery
Mr Stranglehold, gym

Welcome!

Vandalism

Unfortunately, our school has suffered a great
deal from vandalism over the last few weeks. The
culprits have not yet been apprehended. Bicycle
shed windows have been broken and the flower
tubs have been overturned.
If anyone has any information at all about this,
he or she should contact Mr Caries the janitor.

Cups

As you know, our school is constantly trying to improve the environment. For this reason, no more plastic cups will be supplied for the coffee and tea machine. New cups and glasses are available instead. This means that your co-operation will be necessary to keep the canteen and the rest of the school tidy. Bring your cups back to the canteen when you're finished using them. There are racks next to the door where you can leave them. Help improve the environment!

Video

Our video club is in the process of organising a new video evening with two modern British films. At the moment of going to print, it is not yet known which films will be shown. Watch the Notice board for further details. The video evening will be on Friday the 27th of May. The entry fee will be £1.50 as usual.

The next school magazine

The next school magazine will appear on Tuesday the 14th of June. All articles are welcome, preferably typed. Deposit them in the magazine box next to class A20. They will be thoroughly read before being discarded.

You may find it a bit boring to have to type so much text. You may type less if you like. In fact, the best thing to do is to type text that will actually be used for your own school magazine. You can use that text to practise the next few exercises.

Save the text just to be sure you won't lose it.

☞ Click on the **File** menu.
☞ Click on **Save As**.
☞ Give a suitable name, MAGAZ.DOC for instance.
☞ Choose the C:\TEXT directory.
☞ Click on **OK**.

Click on the **OK** button when the **Summary Info** dialog box appears.

Layout of the title and headlines

Now that you have typed all the text, you can begin on the layout. The font and point size are to be changed.

Mark the title of the magazine:

☞ Place the mouse pointer in front of 'The Glossy magazine' so that it turns into an arrow.
☞ Click once on the left mouse button.

The title is shown in a different colour or shading.

Then change the font and point size:

☞ Click on the following arrow on the *ribbon*:

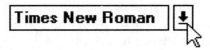

☞ Click on the **Arial** option from the list.

If this font does not occur in your list, select another font which you find attractive.

☞ Then click on the following arrow on the *ribbon*:

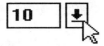

☞ Click on font size **12**.

Change the title to bold and italics:

☞ Make sure that the title is still marked.
☞ Click on the following two buttons on the *ribbon*:

The first button changes the title to **boldface** and the second places it in *italics*.

You can also give all these commands quite easily in one go. Instead of using the ribbon, use a dialog window from the **Format** menu. Proceed as follows:

☞ Mark the title.
☞ Click on the **Format** menu on the menubar.
☞ Click on **Character**.
☞ Place crosses in the check boxes next to **Bold** and **Italic**.
☞ Click on the arrow pointing downwards in the **Font** box and click on **Arial** in the list.
☞ Click on the arrow pointing downwards under **Points** and click on **12**.
☞ Click on **OK** when the box is completed to your satisfaction:

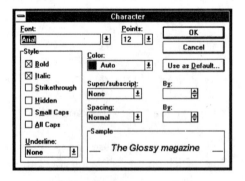

Reduce the size of the letters in the line 'Gloucester High school newspaper':

☞ Mark this line.
☞ Click on the *point size box* on the *ribbon* which now contains 10.
☞ Delete the 10 using **Del** or **Backspace** and type **9**.
☞ Click anywhere in the text. The size changes.

We shall now *centre* these two lines, in other words, place them in the middle of the line.

☞ Mark both lines by clicking in front of the first title, holding down the mouse button and dragging the mouse downwards so that the second line is also marked. Then release the mouse button.
☞ Click on the following button (for centring) on the *ribbon*:

Click anywhere in the text.

There are *headings* above each topic. These should be formatted too so that they will be more conspicuous.

☞ Mark the first heading 'Sports day a great success'.
☞ Click on the icon for **bold** on the *ribbon* (the large B).

Do the same to all the other headings.

Indenting

To make it obvious where each new paragraph begins, we shall *indent* the first line of each paragraph. If you have forgotten what this means, read
chapter 2 again.

☞ Place the mouse pointer in front of the paragraph which begins with 'The communal
sports day...'. Make sure it still has the form of
a capital I, not an arrow. In other words, place
it right in front of the T from 'The'.

☞ Click once on the left mouse button.

☞ Click on **Format** on the menubar.

☞ Click on **Paragraph**.

A dialog window appears. You are already familiar
with this box from chapter 2.

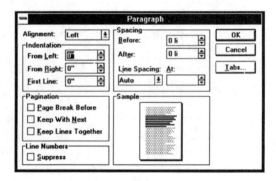

☞ Click on the small triangle pointing upwards in
the **First Line:** box in the **Indentation** section.
Do this 5 times so that 0.5" is displayed.

The first line will now be indented by 0.5 inches.

☞ Click on **OK**.

Do the same to the following paragraphs:

– 'Class 1E ...'
– 'It is still ...'
– 'Our cookery teacher ...'
– 'Since the first of this month ...'

And just for practice we shall use a different method to indent the other first lines. We shall use the *ruler*.

☞ Place the mouse pointer in front of the word 'Welcome!'.
☞ Click on the left mouse button.
☞ Place the mouse pointer on the following symbol on the *ruler*:

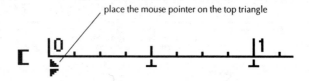

place the mouse pointer on the top triangle

You can use this symbol to indent a line.

☞ Press the left mouse button and hold it down.
☞ Drag the top triangle to halfway between **0** and **1**.

This means you are telling Word to indent this line by **0.5"**.

☞ Release the mouse button when the triangle is positioned at the correct place:

The line is automatically indented!

Do the same with the following paragraphs:

– 'Unfortunately, ...'
– 'As you know ...'
– 'Our video club ...'
– 'The next school ...'

The first part of the school magazine looks something like this:

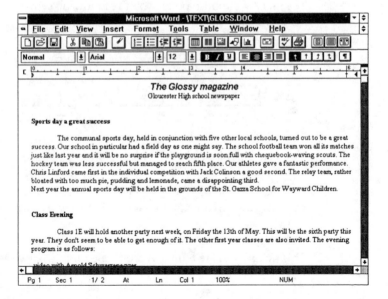

Dividing the text into columns

In a real newspaper, the text is divided into columns. We shall now do that to give our text a
more professional look.

Mark the whole text except for the title and the
next line:

☞ Place the mouse pointer in front of the heading
'Sports day...'.
☞ Press the left mouse button and hold it down.
☞ Move the mouse downwards until you reach
the end of the text.
☞ Release the mouse button.

If everything has gone smoothly, the whole text
will now be marked except for the top two lines.

☞ Click on **Format** on the menubar.
☞ Click on **Columns**.

The **Columns** dialog box appears. Click on the
small triangle pointing upwards behind **Number of
Columns:** so that **2** is shown. You can also just
type **2** in the box.

☞ Click on the arrow pointing downwards in the
Apply To: box.

A list is opened. Click on **Selected Text**.

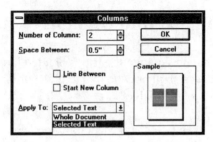

You only want to divide the marked (selected) text
into columns and not the titles because these
should remain centred above the text.

☞ Click on **OK**.

The text is displayed on the screen in *one* narrow
column.

☞ Click anywhere in the text to remove the mark-
    ing. The text is not shown in columns on the
    screen. But you can see it using the *print pre-
    view*. We shall do that shortly.

Making a header

Finally, just to round it all off, we shall place a
header at the top of the page. This will contain the
name of the magazine, the year, the number and
the page number. The name should not be printed
on the first page because the name is already displayed there in large letters.

Unfortunately, our example only has one page; but

a normal newspaper has several of course. In that
case, a header is very useful.

☞ Click on **View** on the menubar.
☞ Click on **Header/Footer**.

A dialog box appears.

☞ Click on **Header**.
☞ Click on the check box for **Different First
Page**. A cross is placed there.
☞ Click on **Header** again.
☞ Click on **OK**.

A header window appears just like the one in chapter 2. Enter the following in this window:

☞ Type 'The Glossy Magazine - 3rd Year, number
5 - page (page)'

Instead of typing '(page)', click once on the following button to fill in the page number:

The header looks more attractive if it is right-aligned.

☞ Mark the entire header by clicking to the left of
the line.
☞ Click on the following button on the ribbon to
produce right-alignment.

☞ Click on **Close**.

You have now made headers for the pages beginning at page 2. You can only see this if you
examine the print preview. The header for the first
page is created as follows:

☞ Click on the **View** menu.
☞ Click on **Header/Footer**.
☞ Click on **First Header** in the dialog box.
☞ Click on **OK**.
☞ Complete the header window which appears,
   just as you completed the previous one. Only
   in this case, omit 'The Glossy Magazine' and
   the dash.
☞ Click on **Close**.

Hyphenation

There is one more topic which we should deal with
before saving and closing the document. When you
make documents which have narrow columns of
text, as in newspapers or documents with wide margins, it is sometimes useful to use hyphenation to
make the text more regular and more compact. If
you have a close look at this book or at a newspaper, you will see that words are often split into
two sections with a dash (hyphen) at the end of the
line to indicate that the two parts belong together.

The normal setting in Word is to have the hyphenation switched off, but as we mentioned, it can
sometimes be desirable to apply it.

☞ Click on the **Tools** menu and then on the **Hyphenation** option.

A dialog window appears:

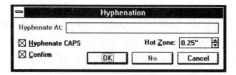

The **Hot Zone** determines just how regular the right-hand side of the text should be. The smaller the Hot Zone, the more regular the right-hand edge of the text.

Accept the settings as they are and click on **OK**.

In our example, Word suggests splitting the word 'conjunction' between the *n* and the *j*. We find this suggestion acceptable so click on **Yes**. Do the same when Word comes to 'try-ing'.

Word moves on to the next word which is to be split, 'organising'. It offers three suggestions here:

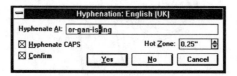

We would rather split this word into 'organ' and 'ising' so click on the hyphen between the *n* and the *i*. The click on **Yes**. The hyphen is placed and Word moves on.

If you think that this is all a lot of bother, you can
let Word do all the work itself. Move the mouse
pointer to the **Confirm** check box in the **Hyphenation** dialog box and click on the check box so that
the cross is removed.

The program will then go on automatically to hy-
phenate any other words which are too long for
the line. When it has completed its task a dialog
box appears:

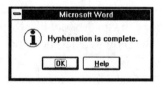

Click on **OK** to close the Hyphenation function.

Saving the school magazine

You can do much more using the Word format options, much more than we can mention here.
Nevertheless, you should have received a reason-
able idea of the facilities provided for making a
real school magazine.

You can try out all kinds of things. You could use
different fonts, divide the text into more columns
or even introduce a drawing.

When you have finished adjusting the layout, you
can save the magazine:

☞ Click on the **File** menu.
☞ Click on **Save**.

Because you have already saved the document
under the name GLOSS.DOC, you do not need to
select the **Save As** option here.

If you now examine the print preview (**File** then
Print Preview), you will see that it is divided into
columns.

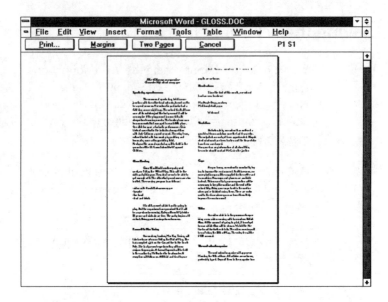

Copying text

We shall deal with one final aspect of word processing which can be extremely useful, copying
text. We shall do this by means of an example
which uses text we have already created.

Make sure the GLOSS.DOC document is on the
screen. It is really still a secret, but your band is
going to play at the party being thrown by 1E next
week. You decide to tell your friend Paul about it
in your letter to him.

Move through the GLOSS.DOC until you come to
the section entitles **Class Evening**. This section is to
be marked.

☞ Place the mouse pointer at the left of the heading so that it remains an arrow.

☞ Click on the left mouse button and hold it down.

☞ Drag the mouse downwards so that the text is marked.

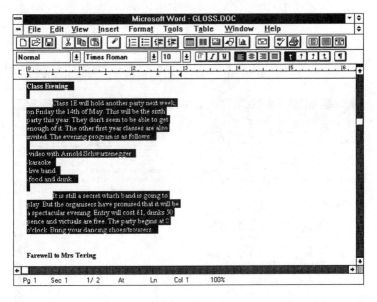

☞ Open the **Edit** menu and choose **Copy**.

This section of text is now stored in the so-called **Clipboard**.

Now go to the **File** menu and select the **Open** command. Open the LETTER.DOC file which contains the letter to your friend Paul. Move the cursor to the very end of the letter. We shall write a short PS.

PS. Our band is going to play at a school
party next week. It was announced in the
school magazine, although nobody knows yet
that it's going to be us. This is what was in
the school magazine.

Type this PS at the bottom of your letter. Then type
two blank line by pressing **Enter twice**.

☞ Now open the **Edit** menu.

☞ Choose the **Paste** command by clicking on it.

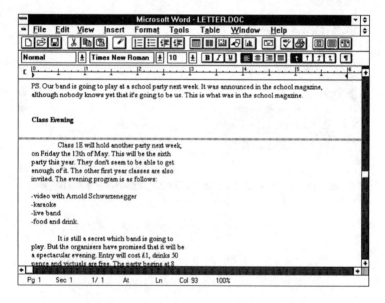

As you see, the text is added to your letter immediately. Of course, this is only an example. But it
does indicate how easily text can be copied from
one document to another.

You can do the same *within* a document if you
want to repeat a particular section.

If you want to *move* the text to a new position instead of *copying* it, choose the **Cut** command from
the **Edit** menu instead of the **Copy** command. The
procedure is just the same. In that case the text will
disappear from the original document. Remember,
you always have to mark the text before you can
move or copy it.

Appendix A
Working with windows

Working with the windows system is becoming in-
creasingly popular. The great advantage of working
in this way is that the programs and parts of programs are all shown *graphically* on the screen in
window frames. Menu options are presented to
you, you do not have to remember commands by
heart.

This means that it is very easy to work with windows. Nevertheless, you still need to master the
skills needed if you do not want to be caught out
now and again. Perhaps you are already familiar
with Windows from school or maybe it is installed
on your computer at home. In that case, this appendix will be a piece of cake.

Choosing a different window

If you are unlucky, you will meet problems as soon
as you start up Windows. The Windows screen can
be divided into all kinds of combinations. An
example of a Windows screen is shown at the beginning of chapter 1. Your monitor may show to-
tally different windows.

To start up Word, you need to find the Word icon.
If it is displayed on the screen, there is no problem

at all. Just double click on the icon as explained in chapter 1.

But the icon may not be shown on the screen because it is located in a window which is not visible at the moment. In that case, proceed as follows:

☞ Move the mouse pointer to the **Window** menu on the menubar. Click once on the left mouse button.

The **Window** menu is opened. This menu shows **names** with numbers in front of them. These are the names of **windows**. The Word icon is located in one of these windows.

☞ Move the mouse pointer to the name of the first window and press the left mouse button.

The selected window is then shown on the screen. If the Word icon appears, you can double click on it and the program will start up. If the icon is not located in this window, select another window from the **Window** menu and see if it is to be found there. Continue until you have found the Word icon.

Making a window larger and smaller

You can do some interesting things to the windows in Word and in Windows. For instance, you can display more than one window on the screen at one time. Chapter 4 outlines how that is done.

You can also increase or decrease the size of the
windows, or move them around the screen. Have
another look at the top of the Word screen:

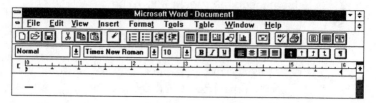

A word screen is actually made up of two windows: a window for the document on which you
are working and a window for the Word program.

In this example, there are two different icons
shown which can be used to change the size of the
windows. To do this, click once on one of the symbols using the left mouse button. If you click on the
 small triangle pointing downwards, the window
will be reduced to an icon. Do not fear, nothing
happens to the information in the window. It is not
lost. The window has only become smaller.

When you want to show the window on the screen
again, press the **Alt** key, hold it down and press the
Tab key. A box appears on the screen showing the
name of an opened window. Hold down the **Alt**
key. If this is not the window you want, press the
Tab key again, while still holding down the **Alt**
key. When the name 'Microsoft Word - Docu-
ment1' appears, release the keys. The document
may have its own name instead of 'Document1'.

If you click on the symbol with the two small triangles, the window is restored to the size it had before you changed it. Click once on this symbol.

In our example, the document window is the same size as the Word window. The title bar indicates this: the name of the program (Word) and the name of the document (Document1) are both shown here.

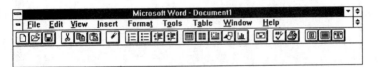

The document window can be reduced in size. If you do this, the document will be given its own title bar showing the name of the document. The title bar in the Word window then only shows the name of the program, Word.

Move the mouse pointer to this symbol in the *document* window. The same symbol above belongs to the Word window.

Click once using the left mouse button. The document window is reduced in size and receives its own title bar.

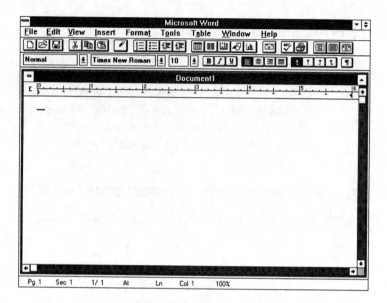

You now see that the toolbar and ribbon belong to
the Word window and the ruler belongs to the document window.

A third symbol has now appeared: a small triangle
pointing upwards. If you click on this symbol,
which is located at the right-hand side of the title
bar (Document1), the window is enlarged to give it
the maximum size.

Experiment with the various symbols. You can alter
the sizes of both the document window and the
Word window.

It is not possible to reduce the document window
to an icon. This can be done with the Word window.

Moving windows

A window which does not have the maximum size can be easily moved. Reduce the document window so that it no longer has the maximum size, as outlined above.

☞ Click on the title bar of the document window and hold the mouse button down.
☞ Move the mouse so that the window is dragged to a different place on the screen.
☞ Release the mouse button.

The window has a new position on the screen. Try this out. It can do no harm and it will be useful when you are working with other Windows programs later.

Appendix B
Working with files and directories

This appendix deals with working with files and directories. If you follow the examples in this book, our intention is to save the documents in the C:\TEXT *subdirectory*

Your computer contains a large disk on which you can save your files. These files may be made up of programs, such as Windows or Word, and also files which you create yourself such as word processing files or documents.

The large disk, called the *harddisk* is always referred to by the letter C:. Your computer may even have more harddisks, referred to as D: or E: for instance. In this book, we are working with C:.

The harddisk is divided into *directories*. A directory is a part of the disk where files are placed which belong together. Just as in a large shop or supermarket for instance, the same type of goods are placed together on one shelf or in one section. This makes them easy to find.

In the same way, the Windows program files are placed in their own separate directory and the Word files in their own directory.

The directory structure resembles a tree with branches. There is one basic directory on the hard disk. This is called the *root directory*. You could say that this resembles the entry hall in a large building or department store. The other directories branch off from this one hall.

The other directories branch off from the root directory. They are referred to as *subdirectories*. Each subdirectory can then have its own branches just like departments have their own sections and rooms. They can be referred to as subsubdirectories and subsubsubdirectories but this becomes too complicated. Generally we only talk about directories and subdirectories.

Each directory has its own name. The root directory on the harddisk is always called C:\. The *backslash* (\) represents the root directory.

The directory structure looks something like this, although the directories on your computer will be different because you will probably have other programs and files:

Examples

–   In our example, 123R4W is a subdirectory of
    the root directory. We call this directory
    C:\123R4W.
–   AFB is a subdirectory of the root directory. We
    call this C:\AFB.
–   LIBRARY is a subdirectory van C:\123R4W.
    This directory is called C:\123R4W\LIBRARY.
–   On your computer, you will see that WIN-
    WORD is a subdirectory of the root directory.
    This contains the Word files. This directory is
    called C:\WINWORD.
–   IN our example, ADDINS is a subdirectory of
    the PROGRAMS directory which is a subdirec-
    tory of the 123R4W directory which is a subdi-
    rectory of the root directory. We call this
    C:\123R4W\PROGRAMS\ADDINS.

The backslash (\) is always used to separate a directory and its subdirectory.

To work with the TEXT subdirectory in this book,
you will have to create it. This directory, C:\TEXT,
is used to store the documents which are made in
the course of working through this book.

To make this directory, you have to give a command outside Windows. The command is given behind the DOS prompt. This is called a DOS command.

If Windows has not yet been started, the DOS
prompt will be shown on your screen:

C:\>

If Windows and/or Word has already been started, press the **Alt** key, hold it down and then press the **Tab** key. Do this until 'Program Manager' appears in the box. When this happens, release the keys. You are now in the Program Manager window.

Click on **Window** on the menubar and then on **Main** if this window is not already shown on the screen. A new window opens, Main. Double click on the icon for **MS-DOS Prompt**. Windows disappears temporarily.

Now you should 'go' to the root directory so type

```
cd \
```

The prompt will change to

```
C:>
```

Now create the TEXT directory. This is done by typing the following command:

```
md TEXT
```

This stands for Make Directory called Text.

You can now return to Windows and to the Word program by holding down the **Alt** key and pressing the **Tab** key until the program you want is shown (at the top of the screen this time). When 'Microsoft Word' appears, release both keys.

You have now created the C:\TEXT subdirectory and have returned to the Word program.

Of course, you can save your files on a diskette instead of on the harddisk if you like. In that case, when saving your documents you must click on **a:** or **b:** in the **Drives** section of the **Save As** dialog box. Drive A: is usually the upper opening where you can insert a diskette and drive B: is usually the lower one. If your computer has only one drive for diskettes, it is called A:.

Index

also in this series:

Word Processing with WordPerfect
be an expert!

Everybody wants to work with WordPerfect. But… how do you go about it? If you use this book, you can find out how WordPerfect enables you to apply all kinds of word processing features. For instance you can write your text in columns just as in newspapers or magazines, you can move whole passages of text, you can even place drawings in your letters and documents.

It does not matter if you have not used this program before - everything will be explained right from the very beginning. And when you have finished this book, you will be ready to step into the world of Fleet Street!

Some of the exercises in this book:

- making an invitation to a party
- changing the appearance of the letters (bold, italics, underlined, size, spacing etc.)
- using the automatic spelling check
- writing punishment lines automatically
- how to print the text.

ISBN 1-85365-351-9

also in this series:

Programming with QBasic
be an expert!

If you want the computer to carry out your own special wishes, you have to program it. This means that you create a list of commands which the computer has to perform. Of course, you must do this according to particular rules, in a certain language. The language we deal with in this book is called QBasic. When you get your computer, you are also supplied with QBasic. Programming in this language can be done quickly and easily. The results of your work are immediately obvious.
When you have finished this book, you will not only be able to write your own programs, you will have also created the following programs:

- a program to make your computer beep
- a program to capture hearts
- a program to play the game of Mastermind
- a program to arrange the sports results
- a program to keep track of your pocket money and to write menus
- a program for making tunes.

There is something for everybody. There's a whole world just waiting to be programmed!

ISBN 1-85365-346-2

Printed in the EEC